HANDICAPPING
YOUR
MBA
ODDS

PROFILES OF 101 APPLICANTS
& THEIR ODDS OF GETTING
INTO A TOP BUSINESS SCHOOL

JOHN A. BYRNE
& SANFORD KREISBERG

POETS &
QUANTS

ISBN: 061561356X
ISBN-13: 9780615613567

Table of Contents

Introduction

It all started with a question.

Over a long lunch at the Legal Seafoods' restaurant in Boston's Harvard Square in the fall of 2011, I asked Sandy Kreisberg what was keeping MBA applicants up at night.

If anyone would know about the sleep habits of hopeful MBA candidates, it would have to be Sandy, known as the HBS Guru. For the past 20 years, he has counseled thousands of MBA applicants as one of the world's leading admissions consultants. He's held many sweaty hands, helping to guide his clients through what is often a difficult journey filled with anxiety and pressure.

And over all those years, he has helped thousands of applicants gain acceptance to Harvard, Stanford, Wharton, Tuck, Booth, Kellogg, and Columbia, among others. Few consultants know Harvard Business School better than Sandy who closely reads every tea leaf having to do with admissions at the world's best business school.

I was asking the question because I wanted to make my website, PoetsandQuants.com, the most relevant and helpful source of information for applicants to the world's best business schools. Sandy didn't disappoint with his answer.

"They're wondering if they even have a chance to get into a Harvard or Stanford or some other highly ranked school," he replied. "Before anyone invests their time and energy to apply to a business school, they want to know if they have what it takes to get into Harvard or Stanford."

Then, on the spot, Sandy suggested a possible story: "Why don't we create a half dozen profiles of typical MBA candidates and I'll comment on their chances." And to make it a bit more enticing, Sandy agreed with my suggestion to actually handicap the odds of acceptance for each of the applicant's targeted business schools.

I loved the idea.

For the rest of the lunch, we scoped out a half dozen applicants and I essentially drilled him on each of the listed attributes: undergraduate grade point average, GMAT score, work experience, extracurricular involvements and goals.

There was "Mr. Near Ivy," the profile of a person who went to school at a great university that wasn't officially Ivy League and who worked in a near Ivy-League organization. He had a low GMAT of only 630 but an impressive 3.9 GPA from a University of Michigan, a UC-Berkeley or a University of Virginia. He worked for Accenture, Booz or IBM.

Sandy wasn't too optimistic about the person's chances at Harvard. He estimated them at less than 20%. But he was much more encouraging when it came to Michigan and Duke, where the odds jumped to as high as 50%.

As he put it: "The GMAT is way too low for Harvard, Stanford and Wharton. HBS would wink at a 620 in some cases, if there were another positive story someplace. HBS admits from non-tier one consulting companies happen, but the stats are usually rock solid and there is a gender, identity-politics story as well in the background.

"At any rate, for all schools, this applicant should take the GMAT twice to show seriousness. This seems impossible at Wharton unless there is some explanation for the low GMAT based on identity politics. Other schools will need evidence that the GMAT is not a fair reflection of his chance of success."

And then there was "Ms. First Generation," the profile of a female candidate with a 720 GMAT score and a 4.0 GPA from the University of Maryland. This person worked at Raytheon as a financial analyst, had average extra-curriculars, but was the first in her family to graduate from college. Sandy gave her really good odds at Harvard (50% to 80%) and virtually guaranteed her admission to Chicago Booth and Duke University's Fuqua School (up to 95% for each).

His commentary: "Her 4.0 GPA as a first generation college grad really makes a difference here. The fact that she's female improves her odds by five to ten percentage points. As always, her chances at non-Harvard, Stanford and Wharton schools depend on her convincing them that she is serious about them, by visiting, meeting other students, and having solid personal and professional reasons to attend."

These two profiles were among the first six published by PoetsandQuants, along with an invitation to real applicants to follow the format and submit their own profiles. Within a week, Sandy would give each of them an honest and candid appraisal of their chances.

Almost immediately, the weekly series became one of the most popular features at Poets&Quants.com. We never imagined how popular this feature would become. We received far more profiles than we could ever assess. And the traffic that regularly flows to these commentaries makes them the most-viewed stories on our website.

It's not hard to understand why. Sandy's insights are often generic. Yes, they apply mainly to the specific profile submitted by one applicant. Yet, his advice is helpful to anyone who wants to crack the code on getting into a highly ranked business school. And his thoughtful commentaries are written with great wit, irreverence and intelligence, making them smart and entertaining all at the same time.

An obvious question, particularly after Sandy has done hundreds of these assessments for PoetsandQuants, is how accurate is he a forecaster? In most cases, of course, these profiles offer an incomplete picture of a candidate. No one knows how well an applicant will complete his or her essays or how enthusiastic their recommenders might be. Yet, as far as we can tell, Sandy is almost always on target, though he can be somewhat on the conservative side.

Consider "Ms. Hospitality." She had a rather low 660 GMAT score and a 3.7 GPA from UC-San Diego where she earned her undergraduate degree in art and communication. She worked in marketing for a well-respected international hospitality design firm, and she had lots of extracurricular involvement in ethnic identity organizations. This applicant aimed high, asking for her odds at Harvard, Columbia, NYU, Chicago, and Michigan.

"Your chances at Harvard," thought Sandy, "are remote." He gave her less than a 20% chance of gaining an admit from Harvard, but he was much more encouraging when it came to the University of Chicago's Booth School of Business (40% to 60% odds), NYU's Stern School (55% to 70%), and Michigan's Ross School of Business (40% to 50%).

Sure enough, she got a quick rejection from Harvard. But she was accepted at Chicago, Michigan and NYU. In fact, the applicant was offered a full tuition scholarship at NYU Stern, where Sandy gave her the best odds, and a half-tuition scholarship at Michigan's Ross, where he thought she had up to a 50% chance of admission.

And then there was the 26-year-old Brazilian woman who had been consulting for more than three years for a global firm, scored a 720 on her GMAT and boasted a 3.5 GPA at Harvard, Princeton, or Yale. The consultant also had a great story to tell: she was a U.S. immigrant raised by a single mom and she had founded a $1,000 scholarship for students of single parents at her former high school in New Jersey. She targeted Stanford, Harvard, Wharton, Berkeley and Columbia.

Sandy told her that "peeps like you get into HBS all the time. It all clicks, especially if the recommendations line up. As to other schools, it is an issue of convincing them you want to come." He gave her the toughest odds at Stanford—just 20% to 30%, while every other school on her target list he rated up to 50% or more. Sure enough, Stanford turned her down but she got an invite from her four other schools, including Harvard, where she will start in the fall of 2012. "You were right on the money!" she told Sandy on PoetsandQuants. "I got acceptances to all but Stanford; couldn't leverage the do-gooder and immigrant back story right I guess. But, as you predicted, HBS came through."

Pretty darn good. On the other hand, no one bats 1,000—not even Sandy. Another MBA candidate with a 700 GMAT and a 3.6 GPA on an engineering degree from a public university in North Carolina asked if he could get into Harvard, Stanford, Wharton, MIT, Chicago. The applicant had nine years of experience in operations with the world's largest oil and gas company. But he was 32 years old, well outside the average for most of the top schools, and he had little extracurricular involvement in anything.

"HBS and Stanford do not take 32-year-old Oil Guys, and the Oil Guys they do take from Exxon, Shell, British Petroleum and Schlumberger usually have both high GPA and GMATs and some added factor about extras or do-gooder stuff," Sandy said flatly. He figured his chances at Stanford were not much better than one in ten; at Harvard, one in five; at Wharton, one in four. Sandy even advised the guy to look into Executive MBA programs or the Sloan Fellow program at MIT.

Well, guess what? The applicant received interview invitations from all four of the programs to which he applied. He was turned down by Chicago Booth, but accepted at Harvard, Stanford and Wharton, which also goes to prove how hard it can sometimes be to predict which schools will like you and which schools will pass on you. Who would ever think that a 32-year-old MBA applicant would hit the Trifecta, with invitations to Harvard, Stanford and Wharton and then get dinged (the B-schol term for being turned down) by Chicago?

After 30 plus columns of Handicapping Your Odds of Getting Into a Top Business School, we decided to put all of this counsel into book form. In the pages that follow, you'll find a wealth of insightful information to help any and all applicants who want to get into one of the world's best MBA programs.

I start with the basics—expectations for the kinds of GPAs and GMATs that largely determine whether a person has a prayer of getting invited to a top school. Indeed, the number one application killer to a top business school is an applicant's GMAT score. Number two is the candidate's undergraduate grade point average. We show you the very latest average GPA and GMAT averages for the top 25 business schools in the U.S., along with the range of these scores for the latest entering classes.

Then, for the first time ever available in book form, we show you what kinds of undergraduate institutions and organizations are effectively the feeder schools and companies into the best MBA programs. Schools do not publicly release these lists even though this information is among the "hidden" criteria used by admissions to evaluate applicants. After all, a 3.9 GPA from a public university may be quite different than a 3.9 from Princeton University. And a job at Google or Apple will be far more compelling to admissions than a job at a no-name firm. We were able to construct our feeder school and company lists by painstakingly evaluating the Facebook groups of the latest entering classes at several top business schools. The results will surprise you.

Next, I offer an in-depth profile of Kreisberg that is both a fascinating glimpse into the workings of a master admissions consultant—and as fun a read as Sandy's own assessments. And finally, the heart and soul of the book: 101 of the most interesting candidates and Sandy's best commentaries to date. These applicants represent a broad spectrum of MBA candidates, each with their own strengths and weaknesses. There are poets and there are quants. There are military veterans and first generation college hopefuls. There are international applicants and there are immigrant candidates. Some have low GPAs or low GMATs. Others have experience at work in mediocre companies. Some have little to no extracurricular activity. Others have consistently devoted time to help others.

My hope is that Handicapping Your Odds of Getting Into a Top Business School becomes an indispensable guide for anyone considering an MBA degree. And maybe it will inspire you to send in your own profile so Sandy can more directly tell you what your odds are at Harvard, Stanford, Wharton or any of your other dream schools.

CHAPTER 1

Getting Into An Elite Business School

Getting into a top business school's MBA program can sometimes be a frustratingly random process. That's because a great deal of self-selection is going on at the top schools. Applicants who have little or no chance of getting accepted simply don't apply at all. So those who do apply, by and large, have at least the raw stats—in terms of undergraduate grade point averages and GMAT or GRE scores—to get thoughtful consideration.

At many top schools, in fact, as many as eight of every ten applicants are good enough to get into the MBA program and do what's required of them to earn the degree. Ankur Kumar, Wharton's director of MBA Admissions, believes that 80% of the school's applicants are qualified for admission. Yet, Wharton only accepts 18.8% of those who apply to its full-time MBA program. Out of every 100 applicants, the school is turning away 61 people who it admits are qualified to come to Wharton and successfully complete its MBA program.

At many schools today the entire applicant pool boasts nearly the same GMAT and GPA scores as the applicants who are admitted. Consider Northwestern University's Kellogg School of Management. The median GMAT for the MBA class entering in the fall of 2011 was 710, with the

1

range between 660 (10th percentile) and 760 (90th percentile). The median GMAT for Kellogg's entire applicant pool that year was exactly the same: 710 and the range, 640 (10th percentile) to 750 (90th percentile) isn't much different.

The same was true at plenty of other top schools. At the University of Michigan's Ross School of Business the median GMAT for the applicant pool was just ten points below the actual GMAT for the entering class in 2011: 700 versus 710. The applicant pool had a range of 620 (10th percentile) to 750 (90th percentile). The actual range for the admitted class? A 650 (10th percentile) to 750 (90th percentile).

As Deirdre "Dee" Leopold, Harvard's managing director of MBA admissions and financial aid, points out: "The average GMAT score for our entire applicant pool is over 700. So that means that people before they apply to a school are doing a fair amount of self-selecting. Going back many years, you would see a much more spontaneous or impulsive decision to apply to a business school. It was, 'I'll apply and let's see what happens,' because information wasn't as readily available from all these different sources. If you applied to a business school, chances were you never visited the campus. You read their catalog, which was the only thing you had. So you had no idea if you were seen as a viable or strong candidate, but now there are so many ways that candidates can do their homework and be good diligent shoppers beforehand."

In effect, stellar GPAs and GMATs are pretty much a given at the best schools.

The difference between getting a "yes" or a "no" often is dependent on how you put your entire story together and sell yourself. You need strong GPA and GMAT scores, but you also need a convincing story to differentiate yourself from the crowd. And you inevitably will make that story through your essays, recommendations, and personal interview. So perhaps it is inevitable that the journey to business school is one that is often full of anxiety and worry: you just don't know if you'll make it or not.

So forget what you hear about declining applications or the eroding value of an MBA degree. Truth is, the best schools remain flooded with hopeful applicants and few of the prestige schools have witnessed any significant drop in applications. At Harvard Business School, for example, 9,134 applicants vied for only 900 seats in the class that entered the school in 2011. Harvard offered admission to 1,096 of them, an acceptance rate of roughly 12%.

The same holds true at many other top schools. At Wharton, 3,761 applicants fought for just 767 seats for the privilege of being among the graduates in the Class of 1984. Fast forward to the entering class of 2011: Some 6,442 applicants were competing for roughly 860 seats. Fewer than one in five MBA candidates were offered admission.

In fact, most people who earned their degrees just ten years ago from name schools wouldn't be able to get through the same B-school doors today because the competition is tougher than ever. This is especially true because of the swelling ranks of international applicants in recent years, particularly from China and India, who are highly qualified and ambitious.

How do you get through so narrow and selective a door? B-schools generally look at academic factors such as your undergraduate grades and your scores on either the Graduate Management Admission Test (GMAT) or the Graduate Record Examination (GRE). They also consider leadership ability, work experience, special talents, background characteristics, motivations, and career interests. These factors are less tangible, and it's harder to predict how they'll be weighed by admissions committees. Any one of them can tilt a decision in your favor. So could well-written essay answers or a good showing in a personal interview.

That's where the experience of a smart admissions consultant can help greatly, and it's probably why Sandy's weekly column in Poets&Quants has been so phenomenally successful. He's particularly astute at weighing these more elusive factors that can make or break an MBA candidate and judging the odds of a person getting into the school of their dreams.

One simple way to judge if you have the right stuff is to look at five key factors, typically the same elements of an application that Sandy will examine in assessing one's odds: GMAT score, undergraduate grade point average, career performance, extracurricular involvement, and application execution (ie. your essays).

GMAT Expectations

If your GMAT score is 740 or above and your quant score puts you within the 90th percentile, you are a highly competitive candidate for Harvard, Stanford or Wharton and a virtual shoo-in at most other business schools (assuming everything else falls into place).

If your GMAT score is between 700 and 730, with a quant score that puts you in the 80th to 90th percentile, you are a fairly competitive applicant for Harvard, Stanford or Wharton and a highly competitive player to get into another top business school.

And if your GMAT score falls below 700, with a quant score that puts you below the 80th percentile, you're outside the window of acceptance for the Big Three. You should more seriously consider schools outside the top ten. All is not lost, of course. There are plenty of applicants with GMAT scores below 700 who win acceptance to great schools, but other parts of their application have to offset the GMAT score—and the odds start to pile up against you.

GPA Expectations

Similarly, if your undergraduate grade point average is 3.5 or above, you are highly competitive in the applicant pools at Harvard, Stanford and Wharton and blessed elsewhere. This is especially true if your transcript shows that you did well in courses that required more rigor and more quantitative material. For classes entering in 2011, Stanford posted the highest average GPA: 3.70. Harvard was next with a 3.66, followed by Berkeley at 3.64, Wharton at 3.56 and Northwestern Kellogg at 3.54.

4

A GPA of between 3.2 and 3.5 makes you a fairly competitive MBA candidate at the Big Three and right in the pocket at most other top business schools.

It's when your GPA dips below 3.2 that the eyebrows go up among admission evaluators. That's something of a red sign at Harvard, Stanford and Wharton, lessening your chances of admission at the brass rungs of MBA achievement. But again, this is a general guideline so don't despair over it.

Career Performance Expectations

Admissions officers make certain assumptions about your work experience based on where you work and what you do. There are "feeder" companies into the best business schools and having one of them on your resume is a real plus. Just as critical, though, is how well you did in the job. Were you given increasing responsibility? Did you have the opportunity to lead and manage others? Did your group outperform others in the organization?

If you believe (and now be brutally honest with yourself) that you were consistently among the top 10 percent of your peers, you are highly competitive for Harvard, Stanford and Wharton.

If your performance is less consistent, but generally within the top 10% to 15% of your peers, you could consider yourself fairly competitive for the Big Three. If there is no way you're among the top 15% in achievement, you can pretty much forget getting into Harvard, Stanford or Wharton—and that's a certainty if you're not from one of the top feeder organizations into those schools.

Extracurricular Involvement Expectations

Piling up a list of membership in undergraduate clubs and sports isn't what admissions officers are looking for. Instead, they're trying to determine whether you are a natural leader and have a heart and a soul—assuming you have the brain to get into a great school. So among your extracurriculars, they want to see that you led organizations and accomplished something worth crowing about. And they want to see that you're not selfish, that you want to help others in need. So these factors weigh heavily in evaluating the influence that your extracurricular involvement will have on your MBA application.

Generally, if you excelled in the leadership of an organization or played varsity sports, you should be considered a highly competitive candidate for any top business school. If you were merely involved in competitive sports or other activities, such as debating, you would be fairly competitive. If you cannot claim to have achieved any level of excellence in your extracurricular involvements, you would be at a clear disadvantage of getting into a highly ranked MBA program.

Application Execution Expectations

This pretty much comes down to how you executive your essays and spills over into your personal interview with admissions. The essays loom larger because they come before an interview invite.

Well-crafted essays that share personal stories that lend insight into who you are and where you are going will help seal the deal at Harvard, Stanford and Wharton as long as you meet the other criteria. You're looking for a "wow" when someone reads your essay, especially someone who has gone through the MBA application process.

You fall into the fairly competitive camp if your essays are highly polished and thoughtful but fail to knock it out of the park. And if your essays can only be deemed "good" or "not bad," you're campaigning for a seat outside the top ten—not Harvard, Stanford or Wharton.

This is an admittedly simplistic way of looking at what it takes to get into an elite MBA program, but it's roughly the formula Sandy follows when he evaluates applicant profiles.

Above all, hedge your bets by applying to half a dozen or so schools—and try to apply as early as you can. Most schools list their final deadline for admissions between March 1 and June 1. But you can be at a disadvantage if you send in your application so late in the game. Obviously, applying in the very first round means that a school has yet to fill a single seat in the class. So a school can accept you on your individual merits–without much regard to balancing the class with a certain percentage of consultants and bankers and international students.

Over the years, application deadlines have gotten earlier and earlier. The early admissions deadline at Dartmouth College's Tuck School of Business and MIT's Sloan School is now in late October for admission the following fall. Applicants who apply early to Columbia Business School—in early October—have a significant advantage over those who apply later. For the 2012-2013 application cycle, Harvard moved up its round one deadline to the earliest date ever, Sept. 24th.

If you can't make those early deadlines, you're hardly alone. Business schools typically receive the most applications in the second round. Harvard, Stanford and Wharton's second round deadline is in early January. Our best advice is to finish your application by yearend to gain admission for the fall semester or quarter.

Whenever you hit the send button, make sure you feel that your application is the best you can make it. It's not worth rushing the process. Your application should represent your best possible self. Nothing less.

And remember this: the hardest part of business school is getting in.

CHAPTER 2

GPAs & GMATs:
Numbers Worth Fighting For

The most reliable indicator of whether you can get into an MBA program at a top business school typically rests with two numbers: Your undergraduate grade point avearage and your GMAT or GRE score. The better those two numbers, the better your chances are of getting into a highly ranked program.

It's as simple as that. Yes, there's lots more to an application than those two raw scores, but if you don't fall within the ranges of each school's accepted GMATs and GPAs, your chances narrow considerably. And as Sandy says, "The biggest 20 GMAT points in the world are those between a 660 and a 680. Into that valley of death ride many of the folks with 600 GMAT scores."

If you want to get into Stanford, that pretty much means you need to have a GPA between 3.36 and 3.97 on a 4.0-scale and a GMAT score between 680 and 770 on an 800-scale. Those are the 10th and 90th percentile numbers for the Stanford class that entered in the fall of 2011. Few schools publish the full range, though Harvard Business School is an exception. At HBS, the latest entering class had members with GMATs as low as 490 and as high as 790, though your chances of getting into Harvard with a GMAT below 700 are awfully slim.

If you want to get into Northwestern's Kellogg School, you'll essentially need to have a GPA between 3.19 and 3.88 and a GMAT within the range of 660 and 760 (see table for the top 25 school numbers).

THE NUMBER ONE MBA APPLICATION KILLER?
A LOW GMAT OR GRE SCORE

No matter what admission officials or consultants say, this is unfortunately one of the unshakeable truths of the B-school admissions game. Indeed, a 2011 survey by Kaplan Test Prep of B-school admissions officers showed that a low GMAT or GRE score is the single biggest reason why business schools ding MBA applicants. The survey found that 58% of some 265 responding admissions staffers said that a weak score on the Graduate Management Admission Test (GMAT) or the Graduate Record Examination (GRE) is the biggest application killer. That was up ten full percentage points from Kaplan's previous survey in 2010.

A low undergraduate GPA placed second at 24%, while the lack of relevant work experience followed at just 12%.

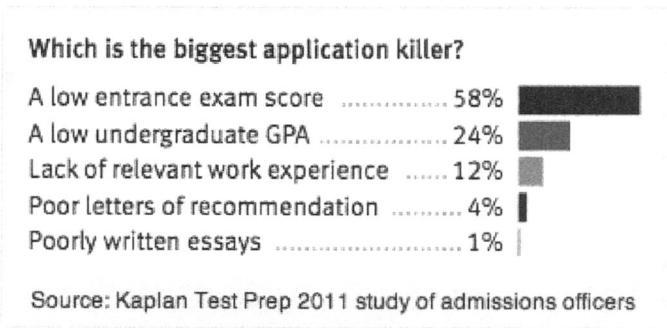

Which is the biggest application killer?

A low entrance exam score	58%
A low undergraduate GPA	24%
Lack of relevant work experience	12%
Poor letters of recommendation	4%
Poorly written essays	1%

Source: Kaplan Test Prep 2011 study of admissions officers

While this fact is hardly surprising to most business school observers, admissions officials tend to downplay the importance of any one piece of the MBA application. However, the Kaplan report, which includes responses from the admissions offices at 16 of the top 25 U.S. business schools, confirms that an applicant's GMAT or GRE score far outweighs consideration of any other factor in a candidate's chances.

WHY YOUR GMAT OR GRE SCORE
LOOMS SO LARGE IN AN MBA APPLICATION

One likely reason for the GMAT or GRE's outsized importance is that it is a recent objective measure of an applicant's ability to tackle the academics of an MBA program. Another likely reason is that an entering class's average GMAT score is heavily weighted in rankings of business schools by U.S. News & World Report, The Financial Times, and The Economist. So some admissions offices often are under pressure to keep those scores as high as possible.

Generally, these scores are highly correlated with a school's given ranking because they are the easiest and most visible way to measure the quality of the MBA candidates enrolled in an MBA program.

GMAT Scores For The Top Business Schools

Rank and School	GMAT Average	GMAT Range**	GPA Average	GPA Range*
1. Harvard Business School	724	490 – 790*	3.66	NA
2. Stanford GSB	730	680 – 770	3.70	3.36 – 3.97
3. Chicago (Booth)	719	670 – 760	3.52	3.08 – 3.90
4. UPenn (Wharton)	718	680 – 760	3.56	3.18 – 3.87
5. Columbia	716	680 – 760	3.50	3.00 – 3.80
5. MIT (Sloan)	710	660 – 750	3.51	3.10 – 3.86
7. Northwestern (Kellogg)	712	660 – 760	3.54	3.19 – 3.88
8. Dartmouth (Tuck)	718	660 – 760	3.52	3.20 – 3.84
9. Berkeley (Haas)	715	675 – 750	3.64	3.39 – 3.90
10. Duke (Fuqua)	689	630 – 740	3.44	3.06 – 3.79
11. Virginia (Darden)	701	643 – 750	3.40	3.00 – 3.80
12. Michigan (Ross)	703	650 – 750	3.40	3.00 – 3.80
13. Cornell (Johnson)	691	630 – 740	3.29	2.78 – 3.77
14. Yale School of Mgt.	719	680 – 760	3.52	3.10 – 3.87
15. New York (Stern)	719	670 – 760	3.42	3.02 – 3.79
16. UCLA (Anderson)	704	650 – 750	3.50	3.20 – 3.86
17. Carnegie Mellon (Tepper)	686	620 – 740	3.35	2.73 – 3.84
18. UNC (Kenan-Flagler)	689	630 – 740	3.31	2.80 – 3.80
19. Texas-Austin (McCombs)	692	640 – 740	3.43	2.87 – 3.85
20. Emory (Goizueta)	681	610 – 730	3.30	2.68 – 3.70
21. Indiana (Kelley)	670	590 – 730	3.32	2.80 – 3.78
22. USC (Marshall)	687	630 – 740	3.30	2.93 – 3.74
23. Georgetown (McDonough)	686	640 – 730	3.31	2.85 – 3.78
24. Wisconsin-Madison	680	630 – 730	3.33	2.79 – 3.80
25. Vanderbilt (Owen)	695	640 – 760	3.40	2.90 – 3.90

Source: Poets&Quants' 2011 Ranking of the Best Business Schools and School Reported Data to U.S. News & World Report for classes entering in the fall of 2011

Notes: ** Reported ranges for both GMAT and GPA are the 10th and 90th percentile.
* Full range of GMAT scores

CHAPTER 3

Feeder Schools To Elite Business Schools

Though B-school admissions officers are unlikely to admit it, the pedigree of one's undergraduate degree can be an important factor used to decide whether to admit or deny an applicant. Unlike GMAT scores or grade point averages, however, it's one of the more mysterious factors because no B-school publicly discloses the colleges attended by admits. Yet, the school where an applicant earned his or her bachelor's degree can loom large in an admissions decision, often given far more consideration than most admissions directors are willing to concede.

Why? Because an undergraduate degree from a prestigious undergraduate institution means that the person was already able to get through a tight admission screen. Many of these elite institutions are natural conduits to the top, including the top of the business school hierarchy. Put a Yale or Dartmouth on your app and there is a presumption that you have already forged powerful connections and are on a track to success.

For a B-school admissions officer, taking an applicant from Princeton or Yale with a 3.8 GPA, after all, is far less risky than accepting a candidate from the University of Minnesota or Penn State with a 3.8.

To get a handle on this X factor, PoetsandQuants collected the data from the Facebook pages for newly entering classes at several top business schools, including Harvard, Wharton, Chicago, Columbia, and Dartmouth College's Tuck School of Business.

What we discovered surprised us: Perhaps the best way to get into Harvard Business School is to already have studied at Harvard University. And if you didn't have the opportunity to collect an undergraduate degree from Harvard, then it would probably help greatly if you went to Stanford, Penn, Yale, or Columbia University.

At the very least, those prestigious institutions are the top five feeder colleges for HBS's incoming Class of 2013, according to the analysis of Facebook profiles by PoetsandQuants. Harvard undergrads make up 9.4% of the class with an estimated 86 MBA candidates out of an incoming class of 918 students. Together, all five schools account for 26.7% of the entire class.

About 30% of Harvard B-school's incoming class this fall hail from one of the original eight Ivy League schools (slightly less than Wharton's 33.1%). Subtract out the international schools in the sample and those eight institutions account for roughly 38% of Harvard's entire class (versus 44% at Wharton).

The data was collected from the Facebook page for the Class of 2013. Poets&Quants was able to identify and confirm the undergraduate backgrounds of some 638 members of the group. We then used that sample to estimate the number of students from any one institution in the full class of 918 first-year MBAs.

While the information is eye opening, it's difficult to draw firm conclusions from the data. For one thing, it's a slightly incomplete sample. For another, it's only for the incoming class in 2011 (though we do believe this data will hold up over time). And finally, it's not known with certainty how reflective the sample of admits might be with the entire applicant pool.

Regardless, buried in all this information are some compelling factoids and insights. And there is no doubt that if you have an undergraduate degree from one of these feeder colleges, you'll have an important advantage in the business school game.

Top Feeder Colleges to Harvard Business School

Harvard Business School's Top Feeder Colleges	Estimated % of Class of 2013	Estimated Number in Class of 2013	Number Found in Facebook
1. Harvard University	9.4%	86	60
2. Stanford University	5.3%	49	34
3. UPenn	4.9%	45	31
4. Yale University	4.1%	37	26
5. Columbia University	3.0%	27	19
6. Princeton University	2.8%	26	18
7. Dartmouth College	2.7%	24	17
8. Duke University	2.5%	23	16
8. UC-Berkeley	2.5%	23	16
10. MIT	2.2%	20	14
11. Georgetown	1.7%	16	11
11. Indian Institute of Tech	1.7%	16	11
13. Cornell University	1.6%	14	10
13. Brown University	1.6%	14	10
15. New York University	1.4%	13	9
15. U.S. Military Academy	1.4%	13	9
17. Brigham Young	1.3%	12	8
18. Northwestern University	1.1%	10	7

18. University of Virginia	1.1%	10	7
20. University of Illinois	1.0%	9	6
20. University of Texas	1.0%	9	6
20. University of Michigan	1.0%	9	6
20. Carnegie Mellon	1.0%	9	6
20. Cambridge University	1.0%	9	6
20. UCLA	1.0%	9	6
20. Oxford University	1.0%	9	6

Source: These numbers are calculated from Harvard Business School's Class of 2013 Facebook page. The educational backgrounds of 638 members for the incoming class of 918 could be verified by Poets&Quants. The estimate of students from a specific undergraduate institution is based on the percentage of the confirmed sample who have graduated from that school. Data compiled by Liza Rodler.

Top Feeder Colleges to Stanford's Graduate School of Business

Stanford GSB Top Feeder Colleges	Estimated % of Class of 2013	Estimated Number in Class of 2013	Number Found in LinkedIn
1. Stanford University	7.4%	30	20
2. UPenn	6.3%	25	17
3. Yale University	5.9%	23	16
4. Harvard College	5.2%	21	14
5. University of Virginia	3.0%	12	8
6. Dartmouth College	2.6%	10	7
6. UC-Berkeley	2.6%	10	7
6. Indian Institute of Tech	2.6%	10	7
9. Duke University	2.2%	9	6
9. UTexas-Austin	2.2%	9	6
11. Princeton	1.9%	7	5
11. MIT	1.9%	7	5
11. Northwestern University	1.9%	7	5
11. UCLA	1.9%	7	5
15. Cornell	1.5%	6	4
16. Brown	1.1%	4	3
16. U.S. Military Academy	1.1%	4	3

16. UNC-Chapel Hill	1.1%	4	3
16. Peking University	1.1%	4	3
16. New Economic School	1.1%	4	3
21. Brigham Young	0.7%	3	2
21. Cambridge University	0.7%	3	2
21. Columbia University	0.7%	3	2
21. Haverford	0.7%	3	2
21. Rice University	0.7%	3	2
21. Wellesley	0.7%	3	2
21. Williams	0.7%	3	2
21. New South Wales	0.7%	3	2
21. University of Notre Dame	0.7%	3	2

Source: These numbers for Stanford's Graduate School of Business' Class of 2013 are calculated from LinkedIn, Facebook and other online sources, including employer websites. The educational backgrounds of 269 of the 397 enrolled students were confirmed by Poets&Quants using Internet searches. The estimate of students with work experience at a specific firm is based on the percentage of the confirmed sample who have worked for that employer.

Top Feeder Colleges To Wharton

Wharton's Top Feeder Schools	Estimated % of Class of 2013	Estimated Number in Class of 2013	Number Found in Facebook
1. University of Pennsylvania	7.3%	62	45
2. Harvard University	6.5%	55	40
3. Princeton University	5.4%	45	33
4. Yale University	3.8%	32	23
5. Georgetown University	3.3%	28	20
6. Stanford University	3.1%	26	19
7. Brown University	2.4%	21	15
7. MIT	2.4%	21	15
7. UC-Berkeley	2.4%	21	15
10. Cornell University	2.3%	19	14
10. Columbia University	2.3%	19	14
10. Dartmouth College	2.3%	19	14
13. Northwestern University	2.1%	18	13
13. Univ. of Southern California	2.1%	18	13
15. Duke University	2.0%	17	12
16. University of Virginia	1.6%	14	10
16. University of Michigan	1.6%	14	10

18. London School of Economics	1.4%	11	8
18. Indian Institute of Technology	1.3%	11	8
18. New York University	1.3%	11	8
18. UCLA	1.3%	11	8
22. Georgia Institute of Tech	1.1%	10	7
23. Williams College	1.0%	8	6
24. University of Texas	1.0%	8	6
24. Univ. of Western Ontario	1.0%	8	6
24. National Univ. of Singapore	1.0%	8	6

Source: These numbers are calculated from Wharton's Class of 2013 Facebook page. The educational backgrounds of 613 of those students were confirmed via Facebook, LinkedIn, or other social networks. The estimate of students with undergraduate degrees from a specific institution is based on the percentage of the confirmed sample with degrees from that university. Data compiled by Liza Rodler.

Top Feeder Colleges to Chicago Booth

Top Feeder Colleges to Chicago Booth	Estimated % of Class of 2013	Estimated Number in Class of 2013	Number Found in Facebook
1. Northwestern University	4.2%	24	20
2. Duke University	3.0%	17	14
2. Indian Institute of Tech	3.0%	17	14
3. UC-Berkeley	2.5%	15	12
3. UPenn	2.5%	15	12
6. Georgetown	2.3%	13	11
7. University of Chicago	2.1%	12	10
8. Yale University	1.9%	11	9
9. University of Michigan	1.7%	10	8
9. University of Wisconsin	1.7%	10	8
11. Harvard College	1.5%	9	7
11. University of Virginia	1.5%	9	7
11. Vanderbilt University	1.5%	9	7
14. Brown University	1.3%	7	6
14. Boston College	1.3%	7	6
14. Dartmouth College	1.3%	7	6
14. University of Illinois	1.3%	7	6
14. University of Notre Dame	1.3%	7	6

14. Princeton University	1.3%	7	6
14. UCLA	1.3%	7	6
14. University of Texas	1.3%	7	6
22. Fudan University	1.1%	6	5
22. Johns Hopkins	1.1%	6	5
22. MIT	1.1%	6	5
22. University of Georgia	1.1%	6	5
22. Washington University	1.1%	6	5
22. Yonsei University	1.1%	6	5
28. Boston University	0.8%	5	4
28. Brigham Young	0.8%	5	4
28. Carnegie Mellon	0.8%	5	4
28. Columbia University	0.8%	5	4
28. Nat'l Univ. of Singapore	0.8%	5	4
28. New York University	0.8%	5	4
28. Ohio State University	0.8%	5	4
28. Stanford University	0.8%	5	4
28. Tufts University	0.8%	5	4

Source: These numbers are calculated from the University of Chicago's Booth School of Business Class of 2013 Facebook page. There are some 545 members of the Facebook group. After eliminating members who are not in the Class of 2013, the undergraduate backgrounds of 474 students of the incoming class of 575 was verified by Poets&Quants using Facebook, LinkedIn and other social media sources. The sample size represents 82.4% of the entire class, an exceptionally high sample size. The estimate of students from a specific school are based on the percentage of the confirmed sample who have come from that university.

Top Feeder Colleges to Columbia Business School

Top Feeder Colleges to Columbia Business School	Estimated % of Class of 2013	Estimated Number in Class of 2013	Number Found in Facebook
1. UPenn	4.8%	31	22
2. Columbia	4.6%	30	21
3. Duke	3.1%	20	14
4. Georgetown	2.8%	18	13
5. Harvard	2.4%	15	11
5. Cornell	2.4%	15	11
5. Michigan	2.4%	15	11
5. UC-Berkeley	2.4%	15	11
9. Dartmouth	2.2%	14	10
10. New York University	2.0%	13	9
10. Princeton	2.0%	13	9
10. University of Virginia	2.0%	13	9
13. West Point	1.8%	12	8
14. Yale	1.5%	10	7
15. Brown	1.3%	8	6
15. Northwestern	1.3%	8	6
15. Washington University	1.3%	8	6
15. Williams	1.3%	8	6

19. McGill University	1.1%	7	5
19. Seoul	1.1%	7	5
19. UCLA	1.1%	7	5
19. Texas-Austin	1.1%	7	5
19. Boston University	1.1%	7	5
19. Southern California	1.1%	7	5
19. Stanford	1.1%	7	5
19. University of Maryland	1.1%	7	5
27. Penn State	0.9%	6	4
27. University of Illinois	0.9%	6	4
27. Amherst	0.9%	6	4
27. Purdue	0.9%	6	4

Source: These numbers are calculated from Columbia Business School's Class of 2013 Facebook page. The undergraduate backgrounds of 457 members of the incoming class of some 645 students could be verified by Poets&Quants using Facebook, LinkedIn and other social media sources. The sample size represents 71% of the entire class, an exceptionally high sample size. The estimate of students from a specific school are based on the percentage of the confirmed sample who have come from that university. Data compiled by Liza Rodler.

Top Feeder Colleges to Dartmouth's Tuck School of Business

Top Feeder Colleges to the Tuck School	Estimated % of Class of 2013	Estimated Number in Class of 2013	Number Found in Facebook
1. Middlebury College	4.1%	11	10
2. Duke University	3.3%	9	8
3. Bowdoin College	2.4%	6	6
3. Dartmouth College	2.4%	6	6
3. Harvard University	2.4%	6	6
6. Boston College	1.9%	5	5
6. Colby College	1.9%	5	5
6. Columbia University	1.9%	5	5
6. Cornell University	1.9%	5	5
6. UPenn	1.9%	5	5
6. Williams College	1.9%	5	5
6. Shanghai Jiao Tong Univ.	1.9%	5	5
13. Georgetown University	1.6%	4	4
13. Indian Institute of Tech	1.6%	4	4
13. Bates College	1.6%	4	4
13. Yonsei University	1.6%	4	4
17. Brigham Young	1.3%	3	3
17. University of Notre Dame	1.3%	3	3

17. Princeton University	1.2%	3	3
17. Seoul National University	1.2%	3	3
17. Tufts University	1.2%	3	3
17. Washington University	1.2%	3	3
17. Wellesley College	1.2%	3	3

Source: These numbers are calculated from Dartmouth College's Tuck School of Business Class of 2013 Facebook page. There are some 350 members of the Facebook group. After eliminating members who are not in the Class of 2013, the undergraduate backgrounds of 246 students of the incoming class of 268 was verified by Poets&Quants using Facebook, LinkedIn and other social media sources. The sample size represents 92% of the entire class, an exceptionally high sample size. The estimate of students from a specific school are based on the percentage of the confirmed sample who have come from that university.

CHAPTER 4

Feeder Companies Into Elite Business Schools

How sexy is the company you work for?

It may seem like an odd question for someone considering a business school education. But it's yet another key piece of data that Sandy often uses to evaluate the chances of a candidate at a given school.

All the top MBA programs essentially have organizations that feed highly talented applicants to them. They include the prestige management consulting firms, such as McKinsey & Co., Boston Consulting Group, and Bain & Co. They include the elite financial services firm, such as Goldman Sachs, Morgan Stanley, J.P. Morgan Chase, and Citicorp. And they include the upper echelons of the corporate establishment, such as General Electric, IBM, Microsoft, and Procter & Gamble.

The more powerful and influential the company you work for, the more likely you are to get into an elite business school. "Sexy" organizations today include Amazon.com, Apple, Facebook, Google, Teach for America, the World Bank and the Clinton Global Initiative. There are many more, but you get the picture. These are cool and sexy places to work and they ooze prestige on an MBA application.

It's the same point we made earlier about having an undergraduate degree from an elite college. These companies are thought to be great screens for the best and the brightest. So when a business school accepts an applicant from these companies it's helping to mitigate the risk of an admissions mistake. That's why candidates with the same basic stats but with work experience at a feeder organization are more likely to get the business school nod.

Want to increase your chances of getting into the Harvard Business School? Go to work for a top consulting firm. The top five feeder companies for Harvard's Class of 2013 are McKinsey & Co., Bain & Co., Boston Consulting Group, Booz and Deloitte–all prestige consulting shops that also heavily recruit from Harvard. Those five firms alone accounted for more than 17% of the incoming class at HBS in the fall of 2011.

Also among the top ten feeder companies are Google, JPMorgan/Chase, Goldman Sachs, the U.S. Army, and Citigroup. The U.S. military is generally represented with an estimated total of 23 students from the Army, Navy and Marines.

There are some very big surprises hidden in this data. Take, for example, the fact that roughly 34% of Stanford's Class of 2013 boast one of just six firms on their resumes—McKinsey, Bain, BCG, Goldman Sachs, Morgan Stanley, or J.P. Morgan/Chase. That compares to Harvard, where 17.8% of its Class of 2013 come from those six firms, or Wharton, where 19.0% hail from those elite half dozen employers. It means that if you were able to land a job at one of those companies, your chances of admission to Stanford improve significantly.

Also surprising when it comes to Stanford is how few applicants are drawn from the technology industry. There are more students in the Class of 2013 from Goldman Sachs than all the MBA candidates combined who had Apple, Google, Cisco, Hewlett-Packard, Intel and Microsoft on their resumes. In fact, there are more ex-Google employees at the Tuck School in Hanover, N.H., than there are in Stanford's Class of 2013!

You won't find this data on business school websites or in admissions brochures. Generally, schools want you to think that applying for entry into an MBA program is a complete meritocracy. They're not eager to let you know that certain applicants have distinct advantages over others in getting inside. So we painstakingly collected this data from the Facebook pages for the Class of 2013 at Harvard, Wharton, Columbia, Chicago, and Tuck. Poets&Quants was able to identify and confirm the work backgrounds of several thousand members of the Class of 2013 to come up with this insightful information.

If you don't work for one of these firms, it doesn't mean you're not going to get into your dream business school. But it does mean you may have to work extra hard to overcome what will in many cases be something of a handicap. Don't let it dissuade you from applying to a school you really want to attend. But do be aware that the rest of your application is going to have to be very sound.

Top Feeder Companies to Harvard Business School

Harvard Business School's Top Feeder Companies	Estimated % of Class of 2013	Estimated Number in Class of 2013	Number Found in Facebook
1. McKinsey & Co.	5.7%	52	32
2. Bain & Co.	4.6%	42	26
3. Boston Consulting Group	3.4%	31	19
4. Booz	2.0%	18	11
5. Deloitte	1.6%	15	9
5. Google	1.6%	15	9
5. J.P. Morgan/Chase	1.6%	15	9
8. Goldman Sachs	1.4%	13	8
8. U.S. Army	1.4%	13	8
10. Citigroup	1.2%	11	7
11. Microsoft	1.1%	10	6
11. Morgan Stanley	1.1%	10	6
13. Blackstone Group	0.9%	8	5
13. Monitor Group	0.9%	8	5
13. TPG Capital	0.9%	8	5
16. PriceWaterhouseCoopers	0.7%	7	4
16. Summit Partners	0.7%	7	4
16. World Bank	0.7%	7	4

16. Oliver Wyman	0.7%	7	4
16. Accenture	0.7%	7	4
16. UBS	0.7%	7	4
22. Carlyle Group	0.5%	5	3
22. American Express	0.5%	5	3
22. Lockheed Martin	0.5%	5	3
22. Shell	0.5%	5	3
22. U.S. Navy	0.5%	5	3
22. U.S. Marines	0.5%	5	3

Source: These numbers are calculated from Harvard Business School's Class of 2013 Facebook page. Poets&Quants verified the work backgrounds of 566 members of the incoming class of 918. The estimate of students from a specific company or organization is based on the percentage of the confirmed sample that come from that company. Data compiled by Liza Rodler.

Top Feeder Companies Into Stanford Graduate School of Business

Top Feeder Organizations To Stanford GSB	Estimated % of Class of 2013	Estimated Number in Class of 2013	Number Found in LinkedIn*
1. McKinsey & Co.	10.0%	40	27
2. Boston Consulting Group	7.8%	31	21
3. Bain & Co.	5.0%	20	20
4. Goldman Sachs	4.8%	19	13
5. J.P. Morgan/Chase	3.7%	15	10
6. Morgan Stanley	2.6%	10	7
6. Citigroup	2.6%	10	7
8. Lehman Brothers	2.2%	9	6
9. Merrill Lynch	1.9%	8	5
9. Deloitte	1.9%	8	5
11. Carlyle Group	1.5%	6	4
12. Barclays	1.1%	4	3
12. TPG Capital	1.1%	4	3
12. Warburg Pincus	1.1%	4	3
12. Schlumberger	1.1%	4	3
12. U.S. Navy	1.1%	4	3
17. BlackRock	0.7%	3	2

17. Blackstone	0.7%	3	2
17, Caribou Coffee	0.7%	3	2
17. Credit Suisse	0.7%	3	2
17. Deutsche Bank	0.7%	3	2
17. Evercore Partners	0.7%	3	2
17. Gates Foundation	0.7%	3	2
17. Golden Gate Capital	0.7%	3	2
17. KKR	0.7%	3	2
17. Lazard	0.7%	3	2
17. LEK Consulting	0.7%	3	2
17. PriceWaterhouseCoopers	0.7%	3	2
17. U.S. Army	0.7%	3	2
17. Ziff Brothers	0.7%	3	2

Source: These numbers for Stanford's Graduate School of Business' Class of 2013 are cal-culated from LinkedIn, Facebook and other online sources, including employer websites. The work backgrounds of 269 of the 397 enrolled students were confirmed by Poets&Quants using Internet searches. The estimate of students with work experience at a specific firm is based on the percentage of the confirmed sample who have worked for that employer.

Top Feeder Companies Into The Wharton School of Business

Wharton's Top Feeder Organizations	Estimated % of Class of 2013	Estimated Number in Class of 2013	Number Found in Facebook
1. McKinsey & Co.	5.5%	47	30
2. Boston Consulting Group	4.6%	39	25
3. Bain & Co.	3.1%	26	17
4. Goldman Sachs	2.0%	17	11
4. JP Morgan	2.0%	17	11
5. Morgan Stanley	1.8%	16	10
6. Deloitte	1.5%	12	8
6. U.S. Army	1.5%	12	8
6. Booz & Co.	1.5%	12	8
9. Barclays Bank	1.1%	9	6
9. Accenture	1.1%	9	6
9. Oliver Wyman	1.1%	9	6
13. Google	0.9%	8	5
13. LEK Consulting	0.9%	8	5
15. American Express	0.7%	6	4
15. Deutsche Bank	0.7%	6	4
15. UBS	0.7%	6	4
15. Microsoft	0.7%	6	4

19. Procter & Gamble	0.6%	5	3
19. World Bank	0.6%	5	3
19. Monitor Group	0.6%	5	3
19. Bank of America	0.6%	5	3
23. Blackstone Group	0.4%	3	2
23. A.T. Kearney	0.4%	3	2
23. Credit Suisse	0.4%	3	2
23. Huron Consulting Group	0.4%	3	2

Source: These numbers are calculated from Wharton's Class of 2013 Facebook page. Poets&Quants verified some 621 members of the incoming class of 845. The work backgrounds of 544 of those students were confirmed via Facebook, LinkedIn, or other social networks. The estimate of students with work experience at a specific firm is based on the percentage of the confirmed sample that worked for that employer. Data compiled by Liza Rodler.

Top Feeder Companies Into Chicago Booth School of Business

Top Feeder Organizations To Chicago Booth	Estimated % of Class of 2013	Estimated Number in Class of 2012	Number Found in Facebook
1. Deloitte	2.2%	13	9
1. PriceWaterhouseCoopers	2.2%	13	9
3. Citigroup	2.0%	11	8
3. Ernst & Young	2.0%	11	8
5. Bain & Co.	1.7%	10	7
5. Goldman Sachs	1.7%	10	7
7. Bank of America	1.5%	8	6
8. KPMG	1.2%	7	5
8. UBS	1.2%	7	5
8. Procter & Gamble	1.2%	7	5
11. JP Morgan	1.0%	6	4
11. Cornerstone Research	1.0%	6	4
11. McKinsey & Co.	1.0%	6	4
11. Boeing	1.0%	6	4
11. Microsoft	1.0%	6	4
16. Capital One	0.7%	4	3
16. Credit Suisse	0.7%	4	3
16. Deutsche Bank	0.7%	4	3

16. IBM	0.7%	4	3
16. Monitor Group	0.7%	4	3
16. Morgan Stanley	0.7%	4	3
22. Nokia Seimens	0.5%	3	2
22. Societe Generale	0.5%	3	2
22. Teach for America	0.5%	3	2
22. Wells Fargo	0.5%	3	2
22. ZS Consultants	0.5%	3	2

Source: These numbers are calculated from the University of Chicago Booth School of Business Class of 2013 Facebook page. The work backgrounds of 407 of the 575 enrolled students were confirmed via Facebook, LinkedIn, or other social networks The estimate of students with work experience at a specific firm is based on the percentage of the confirmed sample that worked for that employer.

Top Feeder Companies Into Columbia Business School

Top Feeder Organizations To Columbia Business School	Estimated % of Class of 2013	Estimated Number in Class of 2013	Number Found in Facebook
1. Deloitte	4.9%	27	20
2. McKinsey & Co.	2.5%	14	10
3. Citigroup	2.0%	11	8
3. JP Morgan/Chase	2.0%	11	8
5. Booz & Co.	1.7%	9	7
6. Accenture	1.5%	8	6
6. Bain & Co.	1.5%	8	6
6. U.S. Army	1.5%	8	6
9. Boston Consulting Group	1.2%	7	5
9. Corp. Executive Board	1.2%	7	5
9. Deutsche Bank	1.2%	7	5
9. Goldman Sachs	1.2%	7	5
9. Morgan Stanley	1.2%	7	5
14. Google	1.0%	5	4
14. PriceWaterhouseCoopers	1.0%	5	4
16. Cornerstone Research	0.7%	4	3
16. Ernst & Young	0.7%	4	3
16. Oliver Wyman	0.7%	4	3
19. UBS	0.7%	4	3
20. BlackRock	0.5%	3	2

20. Capital One	0.5%	3	2
20. ConocoPhillips	0.5%	3	2
20. EMC	0.5%	3	2
20. Gabelli & Co.	0.5%	3	2
20. Glenview Capital	0.5%	3	2
20. Huron Consulting Group	0.5%	3	2
20. HSBC	0.5%	3	2
20. KPMG	0.5%	3	2
20. Kraft Foods	0.5%	3	2
20. Lazard	0.5%	3	2
20. Lehman Brothers	0.5%	3	2
20. Merrill Lynch	0.5%	3	2
20. Moodys	0.5%	3	2
20. Navigant Consulting	0.5%	3	2
20. NERA Economic Consulting	0.5%	3	2
20. Northrup Grumman	0.5%	3	2
20. PIMCO	0.5%	3	2
20. Royal Bank of Scotland	0.5%	3	2
20. Travelers	0.5%	3	2
20. Wells Fargo	0.5%	3	2

Source: These numbers are calculated from Columbia Business School's Class of 2013 Facebook page. The work backgrounds of 407 of the 548 enrolled students were confirmed via Facebook, LinkedIn, or other social networks (Columbia will enter nearly 200 more in its January term). The estimate of students with work experience at a specific firm is based on the percentage of the confirmed sample that worked for that employer. Data compiled by Liza Rodler.

Top Feeder Companies Into Dartmouth's Tuck School of Business

Top Feeder Organizations To Tuck Business School	Estimated % of Class of 2013	Estimated Number in Class of 2013	Number Found in Facebook
1. Deloitte	3.6%	10	8
2. Goldman Sachs	3.2%	9	7
3. Ernst & Young	2.7%	7	6
4. Google	2.3%	6	5
4. LEK Consulting	2.3%	6	5
4. PriceWaterhouseCoopers	2.3%	6	5
7. Cambridge Associates	1.8%	5	4
7. IBM	1.8%	5	4
9. Accenture	1.4%	4	3
9. Credit Suisse	1.4%	4	3
9. Hyundai	1.4%	4	3
12. BankofAmerica	0.9%	2	2
12. Barclays Capital	0.9%	2	2
12. Citigroup	0.9%	2	2
12. Cornerstone Research	0.9%	2	2
12. ExxonMobil	0.9%	2	2
12. Hewlett-Packard	0.9%	2	2
12. Jeffries & Co.	0.9%	2	2

12. KPMG	0.9%	2	2
12. Oi/Telemar	0.9%	2	2
12. Oliver Wyman	0.9%	2	2
12. Parthenon Group	0.9%	2	2
12. Pfizer	0.9%	2	2
12. Tata Group	0.9%	2	2
12. UBS	0.9%	2	2
12. Walt Disney Co.	0.9%	2	2

Source: These numbers are calculated from Dartmouth College's Tuck School of Business Class of 2013 Facebook page. The work backgrounds of 220 of the 268 enrolled students were confirmed via Facebook, LinkedIn, or other social networks The estimate of students with work experience at a specific firm is based on the percentage of the confirmed sample that worked for that employer.

CHAPTER 5

The Rebel Savant of MBA Admissions Consulting

"Do you want to know who gets into Harvard Business School and how it works?"

Sandy Kreisberg asks the question as if he's about to divulge Coca-Cola's secret formula to a rival company spy. In Darwin's coffeehouse off Harvard Square, the long-time MBA admissions consultant leans across a table with a serious air. He reaches into a satchel and pulls out a thick folder bulging with more than 100 resumes from clients who applied to Harvard Business School last year.

Leafing through the files, he picks up one stained with coffee and covered with his illegible scrawl. "2.9 GPA. GMAT 690. Harvard College. This person didn't get in, and the reason is low GPA."

Kreisberg shows another. "3.9, 760, and worked for one of the hot companies. You want to know what the hot, hot companies are? Disney, Apple, Google. A high GPA, a premium GMAT, a hot company, and he was rejected. Go figure."

The reason why Kreisberg, the self-proclaimed <u>HBS Guru</u>, has all these files is that he has been grilling more than 100 applicants to Harvard in mock interviews in recent years, helping candidates prepare for the real thing with the school's admissions staff. About 70% of those 100+ candidates were in the entering class in 2011. Kreisberg claims he interviewed more applicants to Harvard than anyone in the admissions office of the school last year. A spokesman for Harvard disputes the claim. Asked for more comment on Kreisberg, the spokesman says, "I think we'll pass on that one."

He has never taken the GMAT, never applied to a business school, and never worked in an MBA admissions office. Yet, Kreisberg has an obsessive knowledge of how the admissions office of the world's best business school works. He reads every admissions announcement for what it doesn't say as much as what it says. Every client who wants into Harvard is another data point to him, another tea leaf to read to gain some useful insight to help a customer. Roughly 80% of the more than 1,500 MBA hopefuls he has had as clients apply to the school. Kreisberg claims to have gotten in a third of them, enough to fill more than five 90-seat sections over the years. Another 200 clients have gone to Wharton, he says, while 100 have gotten acceptances from Stanford. So he has a lot of data points.

LIKE A DOCTOR LOOKING AT YOUR X-RAYS

"I can tell who they like," he says. "I can tell what it takes to be an acceptable oddball. Man, I've got a real feeling for whether you're getting in or not. And after going through a resume and asking a few questions, I say, 'here is the verdict.' I feel like a doctor looking at your X-rays at that point. I can tell whether this is cancer or not."

In a business largely populated by earnest MBAs and fusty one-time academic administrators, Kreisberg is the rebel savant of the profession. With his thin graying hair, rimless spectacles and wiry build, he looks a little like an intensely demanding high school English teacher—but few principals would likely have him. His consulting style can be argumentative, abrasive, and occasionally off-putting. Even the seven pages of highly favorable testimonials on his website caution would-be clients of the need for a thick skin. Confides one anonymous customer: "Sandy won't coddle your ego, and it is difficult to hear that essays you thought were great wouldn't interest an adcom (admissions committee) at all. But frankly, I didn't pay Sandy to make me feel good."

It's not that Kreisberg is an angry, middle-aged man who despises what he does. In fact, he insists that he was put on this earth to do exactly this and nothing else. It's just that subtlety eludes him. "I'm the guy who gives it to you straight," he says. "I'd like to consider myself the Jack Welch of the profession, though some think of me as Howard Stern."

More often than not, his blistering critiques come via emails in screaming all-capped letters. To one 20-something whose application essays wandered, he wrote: "THIS IS HIGH SCHOOL, JERK-OFF STUFF. DON'T SEND ME THIS AGAIN. THIS IS CRAP. AND STOP WORRYING ABOUT THE FUCKING WORD COUNT." After numerous drafts, the client got into Columbia Business School.

To another client whose writing lacked clarity, Kreisberg snapped: "THIS SOUNDS HARSH MAN, BUT I AM ON YOUR SIDE. GET OFF THE SOAPBOX, STOP BEING SUCH AN INTELLECTUAL, PRECIOUS, CULTURAL WALLFLOWER, AND JUST BANG OUT WHAT THE HELL YOU DID."

"I was a little shocked in the beginning by his harsh comments," says Kreisberg's client, who does not want to be identified, "but soon realized that his honest opinions were much more helpful than the diluted and vague suggestions I was receiving from friends." In the end, the 'wallflower' made it into Harvard Business School.

TOUGHER ON EMAIL BUT NO BABY ON THE PHONE

Kreisberg makes little apology for his willfully un-ingratiating manner. "I don't think subtlety is valuable," he says. "I just get caught up in the writing. My own mojo takes over. It's a shortcoming of mine. It would be very hard to say these things in person. I am tougher on email than I am on the phone, but I am no baby on the phone. There probably is a kind of person who shouldn't hire me, the person who wants to hear things through a filter. If that's your personality, don't ever hire me."

But many do hire him and many are even gleeful with the result. Invariably, the thank you letters and emails go something like this: "We pulled off the biggest caper of all time!" gushed a client who was accepted by Stanford. Or from a successful HBS applicant: "I really don't think I could have achieved it without Sandy's intense help."

That help doesn't come cheap. Kreisberg charges $2,600 for a full-service package of help "for ultra-devoted types who want to maximize their chances for their number one school." All of it is due in advance, up front. On average, he'll spend five to ten hours with a client. Do the math and the $2,600 flat fee comes to $260 to $520 an hour. If a customer applies to three schools, the bill is tripled to $7,800. The largest consulting fee he has ever charged was $10,400 for a four-school package of advice. For people who haven't used him Kreisberg but want him to look over a completed application, there's the $900 "sanity check" which includes an email critique and a brainstorming phone call. He charges $300 for a "ding report" that assesses why an applicant was rejected, and $300 for a mock interview to prepare a candidate for the real thing with an admissions staffer or a school alum.

A BETTER YEAR THAN A HARVARD PRESIDENT

In any given year, Kreisberg figures, he has as many as 250 clients and pulls down more than $300,000 in income. As he jokingly puts it, "When Neil Rudenstine was president of Harvard University, I made as much as him. That was a satisfying symmetry. And let me say this: As Babe Ruth said about being paid more than Calvin Coolidge, I was having better years than Neil. After Larry Summers became president and blew the whole president's salary out of whack, I'm no longer making as much as the president of Harvard."

Perhaps the most surprising thing about Kreisberg's consulting practice is that after more than 1,000 clients, and millions of dollars in fees, he has only once held an in-person session with a customer who insisted on practicing his mock interview with Kreisberg present. Clients pay him thousands of dollars every year and never see him in person. "Baby, that's the Internet," he smiles. "I found it amazing in the beginning, too."

When Kreisberg, who turned 65 in 2011, began to dabble in admissions consulting in the 1970s, he was something of a pioneer. He started advising friends and family shortly after earning a master's in English Literature at Harvard in 1971. The first HBS applicant he helped in 1974 was a bust. "She had a real hard case to make," recalls Kreisberg. "She was a lawyer trying to get into business school, and as a rule, they do not like practicing attorneys. They figure you already have a profession."

For eight years, from 1980 to 1988, he taught expository writing to Harvard freshmen, while trying to gain his PhD, which he never completed. "I wasn't driven. I didn't have a passion for scholarship." Instead, he earned a law degree from Boston University and for a few years was a litigator at a city law firm, hunched over a desk shuffling paper. He hated the job, preferring his moonlighting helping applicants. It wasn't until 1995, after his cousin built a crude website for <u>Cambridge Essay Services</u>, that Kreisberg made it a full-time pursuit.

"It was one of the few times in my life that I got some place early," says Kreisberg. "I missed the Nifty 50, Xerox, Microsoft, bottled water and the housing boom. But with this, for once in my life, I got to something early." Many of his first customers were from California, early adopters to the web, and most of them wanted to get elite MBAs. As the number of applicants to prestige schools swelled in the 1990s, the industry came into its own. Today, Kreisberg is one of some 500 consultants specializing in the MBA market alone and billing at least $35 million a year.

CHIPPING AWAY AT THE ICE PACK

He works out of his home in a third-floor condo in Cambridge, just an 11-minute walk from the Harvard Business School campus. It is a good thing that he has never been married nor has children. From June until

January of every year, the peak season for MBA applicants, Kreisberg barely leaves his apartment, working his Dell desktop computer and his telephone from 9:30 a.m. until 1:30 a.m., seven days a week. He eats a bowl of Whole Foods chicken soup for lunch. Each day begins with what Kreisberg calls emergencies, urgent emails from clients who need immediate help. "I try to chip away at the ice pack, editing four, five or six essays in the morning," he says. "Depending on what time of the season it is, I may have to return a few phone calls. Leaving the house is a huge mistake. It's possible that from the beginning of August to January, I spend less than two hours a day outside, a day and a half around Thanksgiving to visit friends, and two days off at Christmas."

The typical assignment begins with a conversation about the client's resume and ambitions. Unlike some consultants, Kreisberg is blunt, quick to assess if a candidate has the right stuff to get into a Harvard, Stanford, or Wharton. "I say people like you get in or don't get it. I'll ask them for their three big accomplishments. And then I can't stop myself. I'll say here's how you spin that. Here's what you do. That accomplishment sounds like the other one. What else do you have? Your accomplishment sounds more like a mistake."

Kreisberg says he will not write an essay for anyone. "They absolutely have to do the first draft and every draft," he insists. "People often just want me to interview them and write the application. You get some international kids who think that is the game. In the words of Richard Nixon, that would be wrong. Besides, it takes too much time, it's not fun, and it actually doesn't work."

Instead, a client will take a stab at the essays after some direction from Kreisberg and then the emails go back and forth—sometimes on a daily basis. Typically, there will be three to a dozen drafts of each essay. "The most common mistakes people make are they don't explain themselves," he lectures. "They aren't aware of how they are coming off. They are not specific enough. They are talking in a Victorian diction. They are telling the school high-minded truths. Whenever you pick up an essay and they start quoting Aristotle, you know it's over."

BITCH SLAPPING YOUR RECOMMENDERS

The handholding doesn't end with highly polished essays. Kreisberg gets deeply involved in an applicants' choice of recommenders and how those letters are best crafted for effect. Many of his clients have access to the letters written by their recommenders. "I read them and in 15% of the cases they are damaging because the person either covertly doesn't like my client or the person can't execute. I'll tell them to go back and tell this guy, 'This ain't helping me.' In your own diplomatic way, you've got to go back and bitch slap the guy. A lot of times the guy just hasn't closed the sale. Here's what the guy has to testify to in a letter of recommendation: 'I have been in this business for X years. I have worked with Y people. This schmuck is in the top 2% of Y because of his leadership, his initiative, his technical skills, and the impact he's had on this organization.' The guy has to be willing to say that. Sometimes, the recommender says 'I have to write recommendations year after year. How can I possibly say that?' Well, Harvard expects you to be able to say it. That's their definition of leadership."

Then, there is the interview. Each year, HBS invites about 1,800 of its 9,500-plus applicants for an interview. About 60% of them are admitted to the school, with the remaining 40% getting dinged. "This is an important rule," he says sternly. "Harvard interviews 10 people. Two people destroy themselves in the interview. One is a natural failure, not meant for the case method. Another one just blows it. They are down to eight. Harvard then takes six of those eight people and the interview becomes a piece of the final decision."

Whether guiding a person through a mock interview or demanding more specificity in an essay, Kreisberg, of course, can never guarantee a positive result. "What consultants really do is to stop you from screwing up," he says. "Consultants can stop you from failing more than they can add ten inches to your height."

And sometimes, even a positive result, can bring at least some disappointment. One time, a client who paid him $3,600 for advice was accepted into Stanford, but rejected by Harvard. Though you would have expected an elated customer after he got his Stanford acceptance, the client was puzzled. Why would Harvard turn him down? In this case, Kreisberg concedes, he and his client disagreed over how to handle the Harvard essays. In the end, "the stubborn client" went his own way. After getting a ding letter from Harvard, he came back to Kreisberg for an answer. "Lemme say a couple of things, man," Kreisberg wrote back, forgoing his typical all-capped approach, "You are a super great guy, generous, smart, focused, diverse, and funny...What you needed on these essays was Sandy Kreisberg, the Sandy Kreisberg who usually is 1000 percent certain he knows what HBS wants and kicks his clients silly till he gets it. That did not happen here, and the reason is a mild mystery. Maybe I actually respected you too much to really kick your ass, and call you a jerk and just say, LOOK MAN, MY WAY OR THE HIGHWAY, or maybe you just had to be you."

GOLD, SILVER AND BRONZE CLIENTS

According to Kreisberg, there are essentially three kinds of customers: Golden, silver, and bronze children. "About three in every ten people who hire me are what I call golden children. They are trying to get into Harvard or Stanford. They work for feeder companies like Goldman Sachs, Morgan Stanley and Google. They've gone to Ivies or near Ivies. They don't have any obvious problem. They are hiring me for insurance to make sure they don't screw up. What Her Royal Majesty Dee says about fitting in? They fit in. They don't have any problems. They hire me to make sure they don't develop problems.

"The rest are silver or bronze. A lot of kids hire me and I tell them, 'Look, you are not getting in. I'll help you become an astronaut, but it's not going to happen.' It's some guy with a 3.5 GPA from Cornell who is working at a non-cost center like compliance at JPMorgan with a 700 GMAT and not much extracurricular stuff. 'There is nothing wrong with you buddy,' I'll say, 'but there is nothing driving you in. You are working in a backwater. Your grades are just okay. You aren't going to get in. Your chances are zero.' I've never had anyone come back and say, 'Hey asshole, guess what?'

WHAT HARVARD BUSINESS SCHOOL REALLY WANTS

So what is Harvard looking for and how does it differ from Stanford or Wharton? "The smart advice about applying to Harvard Business School is number one, be a victim or help victims. Number two, at Harvard essays about your work don't score as high as non-work essays, although there are always exceptions. The biggest mistake is that people think the essays are the game. They can harm you more than they can help you. The reason why most schools have essays is that it supports their mythology that anybody can get in and that is way not true.

"At Harvard, the most predictive metric is undergraduate GPA. They put a lot of value on it," insists Kreisberg. "To Harvard's credit, the school is willing to blink at the GMAT. Someone is at Harvard this year with a 520 (out of 800). I give Dee (HBS admissions director Deirdre Leopold) a lot of credit for it. At Wharton, people have been told with a 680 or a 690 that you have to get that up. The difference between a 690 and a 710 has never flipped anyone at Harvard."

Stanford, he thinks, is another story. "High performing do-gooders is what Stanford wants and people with connections. You can do a Dr. Phil number on yourself at Stanford and that can make a difference," advises Kreisberg. "It won't help you as much at Harvard." The difference between Harvard and Stanford, claims Kreisberg, is that Stanford puts much less importance on essays and interviews.

"The discrepancy between what Stanford says about the importance of the essays and what they actually are is greatest. I have read so many lousy applications at Stanford, but they are written by kids who are just Stanford types. Stanford applicants who slaved over their essays would be puzzled and annoyed at how ordinary many of the essays of other accepted students are there. In fact, they would be outraged at how banal many of them are. The Stanford interview is a marketing program. It makes them feel good. I have never had anyone tell me, 'Sandy, I blew my Harvard interview and got in.' People who say they blew it at Harvard never get in. When people call me and say, 'I blew the Stanford interview,' I say, 'forget it.'"

And Wharton? "The interview at Wharton can screw you. If you don't execute crisply on why you want to go there, why now, and what your goals are, if you get lost walking them through your resume, that can be damaging."

Ask Kreisberg what he says to those who thought the admissions process was a true meritocracy, not an arm's race to spend thousands on consultants, and he has two ready answers. "One, I say you may have a point. Two, applying to business school requires you to make some of the most important investment decisions of your life. Going to Harvard or Stanford costs kids a half million dollars by the time the smoke clears. If you don't believe in yourself enough to hire somebody to help, you deserve the consequences of that decision."

101 *Profiles*

A typical business school class is made up of an exceptionally diverse group of people from all over the world. If you're lucky enough to get into a top-ranked MBA program, it's probably not an overstatement to say that your classmates are probably going to be the smartest and most personable group of people you will ever meet in one place.

And that's also true of the 101 profiles of actual applicants that follow. They are poets and they are quants. They come from retailing, consulting, investment management, venture capital, and all kinds of varied backgrounds. They are men and they are women. And they are from every spot on the globe. Very few of them have what you might call a perfect MBA application.

We've organized them by category: poets, quants, consultants, bankers, military candidates, non-traditional applicants, and finally the profiles of international hopefuls. Whatever bucket you fall into, whether a poet or a quant, you will most likely find that the profiles from applicants very unlike you will be as valuable as those that fit your own background. So try not to miss anyone of them.

The Poets

When we invoke the word poets to discuss business school applicants, we're not talking about the likes of Robert Frost or Elizabeth Barrett Browning. We're addressing applicants who had studied what many regard as soft subjects such as English, history, philosophy, and political science, among other majors.

Typically, poets have little to no experience in accounting, finance or statistics and as a result their ability to handle quantitative material in a business school graduate program can be suspect. That's why poets need to show good grades on the undergraduate courses they took in math and science and why they often need to score highly on the GMAT or GRE.

Among this batch of poet applicants is a wide range of highly talented people, often graduates of liberal arts colleges who boast majors in English literature, international relations, communications, journalism, psychology, the humanities, and political science. They work in art museums, in the Foreign Service, in retailing and public relations, as well as in international development and in big corporations such as the Walt Disney Co.

Ms. Museum

- 740 GMAT
- 3.0 GPA
- Undergraduate degree in English literature from a "virtually unheard of" liberal arts college in New York City
- 3.5 GPA Master's
- Graduate degree in art history from same school
- Work experience includes five years at a major New York City art museum in an administrative and research role
- Extracurricular activities include founding literary club, president of Sigma Tau Delta (International English Honor Society), and also some LGTB work, though no heavy-lifting,
- Goal: To be director, deputy director or development officer of a college art museum in New England
- "My dream school is Tuck (grew up in Hanover, was beneficiary of initiatives like Tuck-sponsored project WISE as a child and am eager to give back to my community, have personal and professional attachment to the college's art museum)"

Odds of Success:

Dartmouth: 30% to 40%
Yale: 40+%
Harvard: 15% to 20%

Sandy's Analysis: MBA programs get more applications from the art world, or should I say, the Art World, than many people think. That includes music, painting, theater—and the rich cousin of this family, cinema. Your story is pretty typical, and so are stories of performers who want to cross over into arts management, or have already taken steps to do that.

The fact that you have five years of experience in a blue chip New York City museum, in what could arguably be called a mix of curatorial and administrative functions is a real anchor for your application, and a 740 GMAT is a Rembrandt-level score for this cohort. It will go a long way in having adcoms ignore your drip- painting undergraduate transcript.

There is a serviceable summary of arts administration options and issues (and links), whether within MBA programs, or as self-standing MA programs. Tuck is certainly a maybe, and you seem to be their type and know the terrain. What I would not suggest is your current stated goals: "Director, Deputy Director or Development Officer of a college art museum in New England," which sounds like you are eager to stop talking the subway to work in New York and buy a Land Rover for employment portage instead, including crossing the small stream near your jewel-box rural manse. Dartmouth Abbey anyone!

Also, Director of Development is basically a silver-cup job (high class begging) and for that you would do better with a combination of charm school and a deep network of high-net worth friends than with an MBA degree. Although, sure, going to an MBA program is a good way to meet many of those. I would rather say that you are interested in being the leader of a museum (and not necessarily a college one either) because that job requires a combination of strategy, human resources, finance, development, and real estate issues in addition to your impeccable taste and robust knowledge of art history.

Hope this has been helpful. Fun factoid, and not sure if this true, but it could be. Someone once told me that the total value of Harvard University's museum holdings (millions of objects if you define its museum holdings widely, including science museums) is larger than its endowment, which was last reported at $32 billion. Harvard has a lot of art wasting in basements and they used to have a program (and still might) of lending out art for decorating faculty offices and even houses. Of course, even if true, the art objects are not liquid, and would have to be sold (and much of it has been donated with restrictions against that) but just an interesting conversation piece, nonetheless.

Getting back to you, I think your chances at Tuck are solid if you can charm them and come up with a more robust, and less gentrified, goal statement.

Mr. Diplomat

- 710 GMAT
- 3.8 GPA
- Undergraduate degree in liberal arts from a top private non-Ivy (Duke, Georgetown, Northwestern)
- Working as a U.S. State Department foreign service-political officer, focusing on the Middle East since 2007
- Proficient in colloquial Arabic
- Extracurricular activities include English/Math tutoring in the inner city, an executive student board member while in college, vice president of the student debate team, and competitive martial arts
- Goal: To land a position in finance/consulting focusing on emerging markets in the Middle East and Central Asia, possibly going back into the public sector in a management/executive role.
- 27-years-old white male

Odds of Success:

Wharton/Lauder MBA/MA program: 50% to 60%
Harvard Business School: 50+%
Chicago: 60+%
Columbia: 60+%
Dartmouth: 60+%
New York University: 60% to 80%

Sandy's Analysis: Guys like you get into HBS with solid execution, solid recommendations, and not blowing the interview, which seems unlikely for a State Department dude.

One question that is revealing, as it always is: How many foreign-service political officers apply to HBS and Stanford and Wharton per year, and what are their outcomes?

Just based on your GPA and GMAT and your posting to Middle East, you have to be in top 20% of that cohort, although I realize it is a hard gig to get. The HBS issue then becomes just putting together the right mix of personal and State Department stories, and giving off the right vibe. You deeply seem their type.

Just to clarify something about HBS and GMATs: For our general readers, scores over 700 stop registering much. Her majesty Dee Leopold, the HBS adcom director, says at public forums that GMATs over 700 stop registering at all. Well, we love HRH Dee-Dee, but what she means is, there's probably not that much difference between your 710 and a 730, but when you see a 3.8 and a 780 and some career with the State Department, you just start getting Robert McNamara whiz-kid leader visions in your head. At least I do. Although we all know what a bang-up job he did in Vietnam, that was later after he graduated from HBS in 1939 and blah, blah, blah.

So just saying:

1. Dee is mostly telling the truth about GMATs not super counting over 700 (although it depends, of course, if you flunked some basic math stuff during your wilderness frosh and sophomore years and then get a perfect quant GMAT score, that helps),

2. 760+ scores, combined with other items, like a 3.9+ Ivy GPA, well, Dee may not be impressed, but I am. And that is despite knowing over 20 amazing jerks with those stats. All that said, I've seen a fair number of HBS dings with 3.8/760+, not all of them transparent oddballs, either. Bottom line: Dee Leopold is less impressed by jumbo GMATs than Sandy Kreisberg. Double bottom line: Dee's views about this count more, unless you are applying to the Sandy School of Business, which I do not suggest.

3. Another thing—and this is based on my interpretation of a recent interview Dee did with BusinessWeek and how it impacts you.

The dirty little secret about the accomplishment and setback essays in the current HBS application is that the most important thing BY FAR is the actual setting. A wonderfully dense essay about how you led a team on a due diligence project and got cooperation from other bankers, the client, and peers on your team, which also works in why your leadership was important and the impact it had on the deal and your firm is WORTH ZILCH compared to the guy next to you in investment banking who writes about working in a leper colony and getting the cooperation of tribal chiefs, even if that essay is merely workable. Dee Leopold kind of alluded to that in her interview. It is not an essay writing contest. Mostly they want to know what you have DONE and what seven choices you make about what to write about. I don't want to minimize the rest of it, but once you go for due diligence, well, that essay is only going to be so good, no matter how long you apply the #9 sandpaper.

OK, all that said, many HBS admits write about some due diligence or PE deal, and they expect one or so work accomplishments and setbacks, but the most important thing you can do is select powerful other stuff. That is 100x more important than worrying about how to buff up the banal stuff. Many consultants get this backward, and think that a C setting given A+ execution is better than a A+ setting given a C execution. That is so wrong. Although obviously consultant think, since they can help you more with the execution than the setting.

Of course, it is sometimes possible, for those of you who DO NOT HAVE A HISTORY of working in leper colonies or refugee camps, to make more mundane events shine a bit via deeply personalizing, and that is what consultants can help with—the impact of that help is something I wrestle with. Every year I help 100 or so kids craft hi-gloss HBS applications, and then do mock interviews of 100 other kids whom I did not help—it is always a bummer, personally, to see how little the hi-gloss has helped vs. some kids who get interviews (and admission) with really banal essays in terms of details and executions, but the big pieces are there, e.g. they just got better stories (and better jobs and GMATs and GPAs!) . This is also what Dee is alluding to, between the lines, in her interview in BW, although I'm about the only person in the world who can fully unpack it.

Ok, back to you. This is a strong Wharton-Lauder case as well, especially given your history and goals. A 710 GMAT may, in fact, hurt you more at Wharton than HBS (don't take it over! but Wharton really tracks GMAT scores in some serious way), but man, your story is real solid. Lauder is made for guys like you. I'd downplay the finance part, though, that is not Lauder's bag, international management is.

At other schools you mention, it should just be a matter of convincing them you want to go.

Ms. Retailer

- 740 GMAT (74% Quant, 99% Verbal)
- 3.6 Grade Point Average
- Undergraduate degree in political science from Ivy League university
- Work experience includes managing a $100 million-plus category for a big retailer in the Chicago area with P&L responsibility
- Extracurricular involvement in leading a test prep team for socio-economically disadvantaged high school juniors
- Goal: To help develop a Chinese retail company into a global powerhouse like Wal-Mart
- "I was just denied by both Harvard and Wharton; Stanford and Kellogg still pending. Wondering whether I should apply to Booth or MIT second round or whether those schools are concerned about my quant background."
- 25-year-old Asian-American female

Odds of Success:

Harvard: Ding
Wharton: Ding
Stanford: 20%
Kellogg: 45+%
Chicago: 50+%
MIT: 30% to 40%

Sandy's Analysis: Thanks for sharing. If you had sent me your stats and asked about Harvard and Wharton without noting the dings, I would have said there is lots to like and I would have been very positive about Wharton, just based on them taking lots and lots of applicants like you. Not sure what happened at either place. Could have been execution of application or just bad luck. Both happen.

Do you have any blue chip experience? Is, for example, the retailer you work for local or a national brand? That can really matter. Anyway, let this be a lesson to folks who say I am too cynical. Wharton might have blinked a bit at the 74 percent Q score on the GMAT. But that should have resulted in <u>one of their spooky letters</u>, not a ding.

Sloan takes kids like you and is always looking for smart women. I think your chances at Kellogg are good (but I thought your chances at Wharton were good), and jeepers, you should get into Chicago if you can convince them you want to go.

H and W deny kids like you with great applications, so not sure execution is your problem, but it might be. You might want to have a consultant look over your applications to Chicago or MIT in some quick way, just to make sure you are not doing something really wrong, although I doubt it.

S**T Happens in this game, and what happened to you is Exhibit A.

Mr. NGO

- 720 GMAT
- 3.8 GPA
- Undergraduate degree with a triple major in international relations, political science and Spanish from a top non-Ivy University (think Georgetown/Tufts/Johns Hopkins)
- Work experience includes one and one-half years in consulting at a small company and one year as a project coordinator for a prominent NGO. Have lived in four developing countries to work on these projects.
- Extracurricular involvement starting a technology commercialization company at my university to evaluate university-developed technologies; also taught SAT prep to underprivileged high school students and taught English to recent Latin American immigrants
- Goal: To commercialize technologies and improve business performance in developing countries. "I'm not sure whether to come at this from a Private Equity/Venture Capital angle or from a social enterprise angle."
- 24-year-old Caucasian male

Odds of Success:

Stanford: 20%
Harvard: 30%
Berkeley: 40% to 50%
Chicago: 40% to 50%
Columbia: 40% to 50%

Sandy's Analysis: Dunno, all the pieces are here, including a solid GPA and GMAT, as well as your current gig at what seems like some "prominent" NGO to quote you. Guys like you get into Harvard and Stanford depending on execution, luck, and sometimes having someone pull a string. String pulling is not strictly necessary with this story, although it often develops naturally, e.g. someone at a Ivy-connected NGO knows someone at H or S. It's sorta legit, when you think about it.

The only small glitch is your odd first job, so it's crucial to do a good job not quite 'explaining' that, but describing what you did there as important and elite (in a non-obnoxious way).

Solid extracurrics and starting some kind tech-commercialization company at your university has the potential to be a real plus if you can explain what the hell that means? Was it a for-profit company? Or done within the university? Make that clear!

Ditto as to goals. Maybe it's me, but it just sounds like pre-molded buzz words and not totally in-line with what you have been doing, although it does build out what you claim to have done in college, which I don't understand, either. Problem could be me, or could be just the shorthand we use in these back and forths. But make it clear, and no BS.

My problem is, specifically, don't most "top universities" already have well-established tech transfer programs, and YOU are claiming to have started one? Anyway, solve that problem, with either clarity or honesty, and if rest of application lines up clearly, you got a solid shot at S and H.

You should get into Berkeley, Chicago, and Columbia if you convince them you want to go, and going there makes sense.

Ms. New Wave Digital Creative

- 660 GMAT
- 3.5 GPA
- Undergraduate degree in journalism and English from the University of Florida
- Work experience includes four years split between a Los Angeles-based public relations agency for digital media companies, a D.C.-area arts nonprofit, and now a D.C.-area web design and web marketing company where I am a project manager
- "I'm an admittedly run-of-the-mill creative-leaning Caucasian female with a liberal arts background. Middle-class, both parents graduated from college, and my father did graduate school as well. Both have worked in defense contracting and consulting with big firms.
- Extracurricular involvement in the college equestrian club, sorority [but no leadership position], extra German classes, and a short stint with guitar lessons. I also had voice (opera) lessons and private hunter/jumper horseback riding lessons, and now am orchestrating a sizable charity concert to save a local literary landmark from closure

---

Odds of Success:

Columbia: 20% to 30%
NYU: 40%
UCLA: 40%
USC: 50%
Georgetown: 50%

Sandy's Analysis: You sound more disorganized than you need to be. This is a pretty straightforward career in digital media and just stick with that. Go light on the, "I'm an admittedly run-of-the-mill creative-leaning Caucasian female with a liberal arts background" attitude and just get on message that you have degrees in journalism and English and have spent four years working in digital media, in a variety of roles.

Stop making laundry lists of how white and middle class you are. No one is going to hold that against you. And omit the non-essential extracurrics like 'short stint with guitar lessons.' Horseback riding and opera are OK for some later essay about interests but the meat-and-potatoes should be work in digital media. Stress company and its size, in terms of number of employees, revenues or any metrics that are available, especially if they are publicly traded.

As to current job, and this is real important, WEB DESIGN is a real red flag on business school applications because it often means someone working out of a Starbucks, or some even hipper Cafe, not that there is anything wrong with that, but too often business schools read web design as equal to a "confused young person making just enough money to keep them away from local venue of Occupy Wall Street" but not someone we want at our school.

Again, stress the size of the company and the fact that you are not actually designing sites but are project manager in what I hope is a BIG-ish company. Once you get that story straight, you become possible at places like NYU, USC, GT and UCLA–you could do yourself a big favor by taking the GMAT again and again to see if you can get 680 or better.

The biggest 20 GMAT points in the world are those between a 660 and a 680. Into that valley of death ride many of the folks with 600 GMAT scores: Columbia to the right of them, NYU to the left of them. In case our international and technology readers do not know that famous poem, it's <u>Charge of the Light Brigade</u>.

One could also argue the biggest 20 GMAT points are between 680 and 700, it depends whether you are trying to scratch your way into H/S/W or the schools ranked 7th through 10th by U.S. NEWS].

You are the kind of opera singing, guitar strumming, web-designing sunshine-state lady on horse back a lot of schools would like to give a break to (hard to say why, but that is the way I feel. You ought to link up with a 770 GMAT cheerleader and somehow raise money for charity with some clever YouTube clips). But giving a break to a 660 is hard; giving a break to a 680 just feels so much better.

Ms. Digital Media

- 720 GMAT
- 3.5 GPA
- Undergraduate degree from a top-ten business school with a concentration in marketing
- Work experience includes four years in digital media, web and social analytics.
- Extracurricular activity includes president of my university marketing association, a stint as a volunteer with my school's English program
- Goal: "I want to "get out of the weeds" and gain broader business knowledge and perspective beyond digital marketing, and apply my skills to either a management consulting or product marketing position."
- 26-year-old female Asian American

Odds of Success:

Harvard: 10%
Stanford: 10%
Wharton: 35% to 50%
Berkeley: 40% to 50%
New York: 50% to 60%

Sandy's Analysis: Digital media could mean anything from homebrew web designer to kids at Digitas and other leading 'digital media' outfits, so your job or jobs are important. If you are doing digital media at a no-name place, forget HBS and Stanford. You note is unclear, and hints at two jobs or many jobs, etc. Schools don't like freelancers—just saying this for the enlightenment of the masses.

You also claim 'social analytics' which sounds more like stuff they do at Forrester Research, Gartner and the Yankee Group. If so, that is good but probably won't turn the key at HBS; if not, well, less good. For the sake of argument, if you work for a Blue Chip company and have only had two jobs, this ain't looking like HBS or Stanford. Your lowish grades at 2nd tier schools and only so-so boring (to them) extracurrics will sink you. One important note, for you and other applicants who attend schools where 'B' is not a failing grade, stress that you were in the top 10% of your class some place in your app. Schools claim they know which schools are tough graders, but that is B.S. A 3.5 GPA at Harvard College is basically near flunking out.

Wharton is a maybe, sorta 35% to 50%, if background is blue chip and not flakey. You are just in their muddle middle all around and may get lucky. Kids like you get into Haas and Stern all the time, if you show them you want to come. Do not say you want to leave weeds of digital marketing, although it's okay to say you want to learn general management. DO NOT BE A CAREER SWITCHER. Digital is your ace in the hole. Build your hand around it.

Mr. Value Investor

- 700+ GMAT
- 3.0 GPA
- Undergraduate degree in business from a small public liberal arts school in Virginia
- Started off unfocused and unmotivated to be a doctor, had a change of heart and decided to pursue my passion for business.
- Work experience includes two years in the business management division of Northrop Grumman, then moved to NERA Economic Consulting. Will spend more than two years at NERA before matriculation.
- Extracurricular involvement includes being president of the Student Government, president and founder of the boxing team, and a senior member of a non-profit that has grown to become a multi-million dollar enterprise
- Indian-American (born and raised in US)
- Goal: "I am pursuing an MBA to become a value investor, and eventually to work for a value investing hedge fund.

Odds of Success:

Wharton: -20%
Chicago: 25%
Kellogg: 25%
Tuck: 20%
Columbia: -30%
Duke: 30%
Virginia: 35%

Sandy's Analysis: Hmmm, unfortunately 3.0 could be deal breaker at Columbia, despite a powerful story. They are just really focused on stats. To the extent they take any non-minority with a 3.0, it could be you, since the rest of your story is compelling and NERA is an ace place to apply from. NERA kids get into Harvard and Stanford, but they are usually dudes from Ivy or Public Ivy with better stats.

Can anyone at NERA pull a string for you? That could really help. Wharton has too many kids like you with better stats, so that is remote. Tuck is an outside, outside chance if you go there and really impress them. That place is like a frat rush. You gotta hang around and fit in, but it's a good frat. Booth takes risks as well, although they are not so interested in value investors (nor are most schools. MBA programs don't really teach you how to pick stocks, so that is not a good thing to say.)

For application purposes, I'd say you want to do NERA-type stuff or transition to management consulting. Value investing is just code for you want to be rich. The "value" part does not save you. In case you have not heard, people who say or hint that they want to be rich are not allowed to apply to business school, dirty little secret. The number of admissions to top 10 US business schools over the past eight years of anyone who said they wanted to be a "value investor in a bulge bracket bank" is something really, really low. Could be zero.

Ms. Surf Diva

- GMAT: 710
- 3.4 GPA
- Undergraduate degree in humanities from top University of California school
- Work experience includes four years in marketing (and four successive positions) at a nationally successful and sustainably minded natural products company (sold at Whole Foods and every major grocery store); Currently head of digital marketing, managing a small team of five that executes web and graphic design, social media and content creation.
- Extracurricular activities include an impressive travel record, active in surfing, rock climbing and photography, just joined the board of directors for a surf film non-profit, but otherwise minimal volunteer work at a local organic farm
- 26-year-old, half Jamaican female who was homeschooled until high school
- Goal: To strengthen existing career track in marketing with an MBA

Odds of Success:

Stanford: -20%
Berkeley: 30%
MIT: 30%
Kellogg: 40%
Columbia: 40%

Sandy's Analysis: I've seen kids with your work background get into HBS, although they had better stats, and better extras. Working at a brand name food company in marketing is okay, and it's a welcome relief in some cases because you actually sell stuff that folks recognize and deal with supply chains, distribution, competition, advertising, and sales teams. REAL STUFF. Now obviously business schools don't want too much of that. Because, well, they are elitist and by nature opposed to the reality of dealing with delivery trucks, the teamsters union, price discounts to large stores, sales quotes, and Super Bowl tickets to high performing sales personnel.

Just for the record, consumer product majors like P&G, Kraft, Nestle, Budweiser (or whatever it's called now) Coke, and Pepsi are fine places to apply from. The elite B- schools respect those firms the way an aristocratic family respects an uncle who made a lot of money selling zippers. I mean the money is nice, but it's a zipper!

Your problem is your extras don't seem to add up to much, and the bar for that is a bit higher for kids who don't work in investment banking, since presumably you only have a 40-50 hour week job and time to do stuff.

I'm not sure what 1/2 Jamaican means in terms of qualifying for minority status. Are you a U.S. citizen? If so, you might be considered Afro-American, and that could help.

Home schooling can be a plus if you spin it right as being an important part of your upbringing which created values that lead to your extracurricular activities. The trouble is your extras are all rich kid's extras ("Impressive travel record, active in surfing, rock climbing and photography, just joined the board of directors for a surf film non-profit") so you are, ahem, wiping out with that list. Surf film non-profit?

OK, I don't see this as Stanford, you are just not interesting enough to overcome low-ish grades, unless you do have some kind identity politics story you are 1. not aware of, 2. too lazy to write about in your note. Haas, maybe, given that on stats alone you are not a super reach and there is a lot to like, and maybe even more to like.

MIT? Always hard to say there. They won't swoon over digital marketing background. They might go for a minority woman (they don't get flooded with apps from that group) with a 710 GMAT, if you are indeed a minority, but my guess is, the GPA will be deal breaker. Ditto Columbia. Kellogg is a maybe if you can put together a story. Kids like you get into Cornell, Michigan and pretty much stand a real good shot at places 10 through 20 on the U.S. News list.

Ms. Magazine Journalist

- 690 GMAT
- 3.8 GPA
- Undergraduate degree in journalism from a top public J-School
- Work experience includes year and one-half as assistant editor at a national magazine
- Extracurricular involvement as chapter leader of local alumni association, sorority house chair, co-founder of field hockey club, and member of the Society of Professional Journalists
- 23 years old

Odds of Success:

Harvard: -30%
Tuck: 40%
Darden: 40% to 60%
Duke: 40% to 60%
Kellogg: 40+%
Berkeley: 40+%
Yale: 40+%

Sandy's Analysis: Well, I like journalists, and I am sure John does to, but a sad fact is that people I personally like (Romantics, Day Care teachers, stunt men and stand-up comics) are often not the types that appeal to B-schools. That National Magazine you work for better be more close to The Atlantic than to Sassy or Coupon News. That can really make a difference, especially in essay execution, because writing about working with Paul Volcker on a story about The Fed is a lot more powerful than writing about working with Snooki on a story about being fed. (Once again, more interesting to B- schools, but you can give me Snooki.)

Also, it is a bit unclear what Assistant Editor means, that is often a catchall that could describe many different things, but we wonder how senior the job can be since you have only been there 18 months. The kind of woman with your background who gets into HBS is often Ivy, real high GPA, AND real high GMAT and works at The Wall Street Journal or New Yorker (jobs only Ivy kids get anyway) and then puts together some classy, name- dropping essays, and has recommendations from a big shot publishing honcho.

You may almost be that, since you got the GPA, but the GMAT becomes important because you don't have Ivy education, and most people, rightly or wrongly, don't think a 3.8 at journo school is like a, oh for instance, a 9.5 at IIT, New Delhi, or 4.8 at MIT. Your extras are so-so, there is not a lot of what HBS likes to call "impact beyond yourself" by which they mean helping victims in inner cities versus what you do have, which is helping your field hockey teammates or your fellow journos at the Society of Professional Journalists.

Once we take HBS out of the picture, if you can leverage your journo stories, drop some names, and come up with some legit reason why you need an MBA (that could be hard, don't say to save magazines, but probably okay to say to manage new media projects blah, blah) well, who knows, someone like you can round out the class. So chances at Tuck, Darden, Fuqua, Kellogg, Haas and Yale could be in 40% to 60% range, although your story, your reasons, your likeability (to them not me) is what is going to push you through.

Each of those schools takes and dings kids like you, so execution, showing them the love, and luck really count.

Mr. Coxswain

- 740 GMAT
- 3.8 Grade Point Average
- Undergraduate degree from public Ivy
- Work experience includes a year in intelligence, a year in carpentry, and now employed by a large international development organization doing stabilization work in Southern Afghanistan.
- Will probably spend three to four years here unless I leave for the Navy.
- Extracurriculars include varsity coxswain; biked from Texas to Alaska to raise money for cancer research & started department at university for social innovation
- Rhodes finalist

Odds of Success:

Harvard: 50% to 60%
Stanford: 50% to 60%
Wharton: 60% to 70%
Tuck: 60% to 70%
Booth: 70+%
Kellogg: 70+%

Sandy's Analysis: Well, there's a lot to like including a 3.8 and many 'manly' accomplishments such as rower, carpenter, bike rider, Afghan stabilization ninja. Hmmm, only working in 'intelligence' doesn't seem to fit the macho framework :-)

I'm not sure of your age and timeline. If you have been at an international development organization for two-plus years, with this set of accomplishments, you can apply now.

As to joining the Navy, do you have Seal Team 6 fantasies? Well, who can blame you? And schools will wait, even if you flunk Seal Team ocean swim drills and wind up a regular swabby. Military applicants are welcome until about 30 and even older if a pilot with ten-plus years required gig.

That could be important, because while I am no expert, I think Seal Team Six, or DEVGRU as it known to non-experts like me who read the Internet, is not a three-year gig, since you have to fly up from another Seal Team, and that takes time. Of course nothing too shabby about a gig on Seal Teams 1-12 minus 6 either). Anyway, especially with a 720+ GMAT, you got the goods. So it is a matter of just telling your story as per each application's various nooks and ponds. Guys like you get in all over. In terms of how they don't get in to Harvard/Stanford/Wharton, well, in rare cases it is a massive execution snafu, where, if military, you just tell war stories and say goals are to make bigger bombs, and if USAID, you just annoy people somehow. Of course, at HBS, and maybe Wharton, there is always "sudden death" by interview so prepare for that when you get there.

Man, you are about as "Tucky" as a guy can get without joining the Village People, and it would just be an issue of convincing them you want to camp out with them for two years while chopping down trees, white water rafting and catching up on course material on your iPod while going up ski lifts (or even going down ski slopes, if you are used to more challenging terrain).

Same deal with Booth and Kellogg. You will need some do-gooder/military goal statement about how the MBA will make you more impactful as a leader in context A, B, and C. But those are easy to generate. Just make sure A, B, and C relate to stuff you have done.

Ms. Pink Collar Career Switcher

- 720 GMAT
- 3.7 GPA
- Undergraduate degree in communication from the University of Southern California; also took university extension courses in economics, calculus, and statistics
- Three years as a public relations strategist at Wells Fargo
- Extracurricular activity includes being on the Young Alumni Council's marketing committee, vice president of the Young Professionals Network, and a regular volunteer for a assistance that provides groceries and meal delivery to clients with HIV/AIDS
- Reasons for MBA: To switch careers to investment management; acquire skills to become an influential female business leader and move out of the "pink ghetto"
- Minority

Odds of Success:

Harvard: Better than 40%
Stanford: Better than 40%
Wharton: 60%
Kellogg: 60% to 70%
Yale: 60% to 70%
MIT Sloan: 50% to 60%

Sandy's Analysis: Ms. Pink Collar, come on down! Tons to like, but I gotta ask, what kind of minority are you? I mean—just between me, you and the world, and no offense to anyone—there are minorities, like black women who are the children of single mothers from the inner city, and minorities, like debutantes from Miami who just happen to have Spanish Surnames. If you are close to the black woman with the inner-city story, congratulations.

You have a perfect trajectory. To wit, okay schooling, excellent grades, doofus communication job at Blue Chip Company, where you learned how to fib to customers and government agencies (schools like that! It shows deep business potential), and a 720 GMAT! Plus meals on wheels to HIV/AIDS!

This could be Stanford!

As noted prior, Stanford almost reserves one or two seats for black women from Big Four firms, since it is seen, as in your case, as a "pre-finishing" school on your long climb to the top (USC–Wells Fargo–Stanford, has a nice ring to it). In that model, you are aces. To the extent you are the grand daughter of Cuban Casino Owners who came to Miami right after Castro, well, the story is less compelling, but a minority is a minority is a minority. Soooooo don't go changing your name to Rockefeller.

You should definitely look at HBS and Wharton, too, for the same reason you would be attractive to Stanford. One piece of advice:

You Say: Reasons for MBA: switch careers to investment management; acquire skills to become an influential female business leader; move out of the "pink ghetto."

I say: Don't be talking about leaving any ghetto, got that. And don't say you want to switch to investment management, that is real code for asset management for rich people, and in your case, what is worse, unintended code for "I want to be rich myself." Shame on you! Of all the crazy reasons to go to B-school!

You need to say you want to be an impactful leader in communications, especially as a WHATEVER-YOU-ARE WOMAN, who can help the disenfranchised tell their stories and help emerging companies find their audiences. Spend an hour on Google finding out about folks who actually do that, and say that is your deal. If only that HIV/AIDS meal team could get their story out. If only communication consultants helped outfits like that. There are so many worthy and untold stories. Hmmm, I'm sniffing the cappuccino foam in Palo Alto.

Arcane Knowledge Bonus Point: The only way you could up this profile is to be a guy! It's a little known secret but a real number of minority women have 720 GMATs. A much smaller number of minority guys do. One of those issues no one has the brass to discuss much, but a well-known factoid in advanced admission circles.

Mr. Disney

- 700 GMAT
- 3.48 GPA
- Undergraduate degree in history
- Work experience includes two years at Disney in the corporate treasury for interest rate risk, after internships at Merrill Lynch and PIMCO
- "Throughout college I worked as a full-time student supporting myself, which detracted from some of my involvement with student clubs/ organizations. However, I received a slew of very compelling scholarships and leveraged the experiences from my college jobs to grow and overcome difficult financial situations"
- "Concerned about my history major hurting my chances. But I do plan on taking some extra math courses to improve in the quant. area."
- 25-year-old white male

Odds of Success:

Harvard: 15-20%
Stanford: 10%
Columbia: 20+%
Yale: 30%
Northwestern: 30-50+%
Chicago: 30-50+%
Dartmouth: 20-30%
NYU: 30-50%

Sandy's Analysis: Hmmmm, everyone loves Disney and Disney is great feeder firm to HBS and Stanford, but usually those lucky kids are working in business development or programming of some kind, and got there after some post-college full-time, competitive blue chip gig on Wall Street or through Ivy League friends and family.

As to your concern about being a History major—pal, being a liberal arts major, and especially History, at many elite B-schools is a plus. Business Schools are probably the last bastions in America—aside from the corrupt and sincecured and geriatric professoriate themselves (and they may have actual have doubts!)—that still buy into the now desiccated wet dream that Liberal Arts is great preparation for a career in business.

In fact, professors and administrators will tell you this if you can get them away from Downton Abbey discussion boards or cozy conferences on the state of the Liberal Arts, but I digress. I'm a liberal arts major and it is great training for cracking wise in features just like this, if that is your goal in life. Of course, many Liberal Arts majors at top 10 colleges become success-ful in business, and go to ace B-schools and powerful careers in business and finance. But these are just really smart people, anyway, and the Liberal Arts had nothing to do with it, although you can get them to warble about the importance of the Liberal Arts at any conference which holds out the remot-est fantasy they could score with some buff junior faculty or event planner.

OK, "down boy" (talking to myself), back to you. Basically you're a guy with a lot of high quality silver and not much gold in your story and stats, which usually rules out Harvard and Stanford. Your History major has absolutely nothing to do with it. As noted, that is a plus. What is hurting you is your slightly off GPA and marginal GMAT and being in the wrong part of Disney. (If anyone else from Treasury ever got into H or S, look hard, and you will find something different than a white male with a 3.48 and a 700 GMAT.)

You have a good deal of personal positives. Those and taking some courses will shore up your chances at other schools you list, but will not, I believe, get you into Harvard or Stanford. Getting some mega Disney big foot strongly on your side might help. As would some amazing personal and political identity story, but I am not seeing that in the info you provided. At other schools you list, I would call your chances in-line, both as to stats, jobs, and personal story. You should be in good shape there, after account-ing for the usuals: solid execution, excellent recommendations, luck, and somehow convincing them you really want to go.

Ms. Finance Feminist

- 750 GMAT
- 3.4 GPA
- Undergraduate degree in economics and psychology from a top five liberal arts college
- Work experience includes two years at an old, established Boston investment management firm doing equity research; plus a year and one-half in a Fortune 500 finance training program
- Extracurricular involvement as chair of the local chapter of an international women's leadership organization, active in alumnae network, published poet in award-winning literary journals
- Goal: To eventually run my own investment management firm in China
- 25-year-old Chinese woman and U.S. citizen, fluent in Mandarin and English

Odds of Success:

Harvard: 30% to 40%
Stanford: 10% to 25%
Chicago: 30% to 50%
MIT: 30% to 40%
Columbia: 30% to 50%
Northwestern: 30% to 50%

Sandy's Analysis: Hmmmm, you got gold + silver + poetry. Hard to know how that will play out. The good is the 750 GMAT, the less good is the 3.4, which is admissible but on the low side for Harvard and Stanford. The equity research gig at an "old and established" Boston management firm could be gold or gold plate, depending on the firm and what you do and what kind of support you get.

Let's just say we are talking Fidelity or Wellington or Putnam – applicants from those firms get into HBS and sometimes Stanford, but usually with Boffo other things. This is where your 3.4 can be an issue. As a rule, equity research at Fidelity or another old line firm is considered one cut below pure investment banking in terms of selectivity, although still a great gig.

To the extent you can string together all your women's empowerment extra-currics into a powerful presentation and garner some powerful support within your firm, well, that, and the published poetry might tip you into HBS. Her majesty, HBS adcom head Dee Leopold, may not read much poetry—or she may, dunno for sure, I have not hacked her Lincoln, MA, library card. WONDERFUL library by the way, if you are ever in the area, so is neighboring Concord, especially if you need a rest room, it actually has an oil painting on the wall!!! But a published poet, and your other extras, might move someone off the WL in July, if HRH were in a hurry to go on vacation. So HBS is close but you are in a real competitive cohort so it could tip either way. Not seeing this as Stanford, for all the HBS reasons, and stats and selectivity of employment really count over there, especially since you have a winning but not compelling do-gooder profile.

At all other schools but H and S, I'd say you are totally in-line –just a matter of solid application execution. The key to HBS is just getting some "specialness" in your application, which can be a cumulative build up of little things (of which you have a lot) or getting some powerful fuddy-duddy at your "old and established" management firm to put his wrinkled thumb on the scale.

"Your Majesty, Ned Johnson on line 2." Dee takes calls like that.

You can probably predict your chances at HBS better than me. How often have applicants from your firm who do what you do gotten in? If not much data, you still have a chance because this is just solid and winning.

I'd be careful about how you explain your goals, and what the timeline and steps to reaching them are.

Ms. Job Changer

- 720 GMAT
- 3.6 GPA
- Undergraduate degree from a West Coast public ivy
- Work experience includes a stint with a financial advisor working at a regional independent RIA in my first job after college, mostly in client service; quit job to enroll in intensive summer business program at a top B-school to transfer into the marketing field and then did stints at boutique marketing strategy firm, a marketing research firm, and a university serving well-known clients. Also worked as an online content writer at a tech startup and currently do research and analytics at top advertising agencies for CPG companies, among others
- Extracurricular involvement includes leadership positions in various student groups and honor societies on campus, volunteer at soup kitchen, tutor high school students, mentor young people and am a member of an elite professional women's organization founded by Goldman Sachs executives
- Fluent in three languages
- Goal: To work at a multinational company in Asia or the emerging markets in a marketing role
- 25-year-old female minority who struggled as an immigrant in a low-income neighborhood, having come to the U.S. during her teen years

---

Odds of Success:

Stanford: 10% to 15%
Harvard: 20% to 35%
Northwestern: 40% to 50+%
Duke: 50+%
INSEAD: 50%

Sandy's Analysis: I think you got a solid story here and need to focus on the thread of this which is marketing and advertising to CPG clients (Consumer Packaged Goods, to those of you out there who never use soap, toothpaste, or cereal or those of you who do and just never knew those were called CPG's by insiders.)

The real mystery here is what a female minority from a public Ivy with a 3.6 – and later a 720 GMAT – was doing taking her first job out of college with a "Financial advisor working at a regional independent RIA in West Coast . . . did mostly client service, but licensed and sold securities and insurance . . ." which is a fine job for an ambitious white guy who discovered he was serious about life after getting a 3.2 at a Tier 2 school and his girlfriend knocked-up?

We expect you to be working at some kind of consulting firm or management rotation program at a Fortune 500 company. So that may take some explaining. As will some of the other gigs you list ("online content writer!!!" Kiddo, that is what I DO!!), but once you find your footing, this becomes a solid story of someone who is now in engaged in something hip and traditional. That may be a strong enough anchor to make your other five jobs and checkerboard and odd career not count against you so much. Your extras are better than average, and more than average, so that is another plus.

The confusion noted in career paths may sink you at HBS and Stanford, who have a window for minority females, but prefer them to be really clearly packaged from Blue Chip companies or blue chip small companies, and not have as much baggage as you do in a career path. Just a feeling I am getting, despite all your positives and excellent stats.

One thing you can do at those schools to really better your odds is to get some support from that elite woman's organization you belong to (founded by Goldman Sachs). If you can get someone at that organization who is on speaking terms with Dee Leopold or Derrick Bolton to be your champion – that could help. SERIOUSLY!

Otherwise you are close. I think you stand a good chance outside HBS and Stanford just based on your stats and compelling story, especially at schools like Wharton, MIT, and Columbia, who are always looking for minorities with high stats, especially MIT. But I'm not sure MIT would be your cup of tea and marketing is not their strong suit. I think you are really in line at Fuqua and Kellogg. I would not bother with INSEAD unless you want to work in Europe afterwards.

Your stated goal, to work in a Fortune 500 company in marketing is right on. I would not say you want to work in Asia/emerging markets, that does not fit this picture. Unless you are Asian, and if so, well, I got some bad news for you, that could change this picture a bit, since that is not as much as an in-demand minority as the Latino/Afro-Am/Native American trifecta. Although you have a strong adversity story as well, so that helps in the crazy calculus of B-school admissions. Getting your career path to make sense will be one necessity and telling your adversity story (and perhaps braiding it with your career path) will be another.

The Quants

If you're a Quant, chances are you'll have no problem at all with the core business school curriculum. Accounting, finance and statistics should be something of a breeze for you. After all, you've already dealt with quantitative material.

You studied engineering, math, or a hard science during your undergrad years. So there is little question that you can handle the quantitative stuff that will get thrown at you in an MBA program.

The following profiles reflect such candidates. Even if these applicants are now in fields that could easily be jobs held by poets, they've majored in industrial, chemical or mechanical engineering, finance, molecular biology, or some other rigorous subject. In a few cases, we've included applicants whose major is unclear but who hold down jobs that would clearly expose them to quantitative work, such as private equity. One of our applicants even has a PhD in genetics!

Ms. K-Mart

- 670 GMAT
- 3.4 GPA
- Undergraduate degree in industrial engineering from state school
- Work experience includes three years at the headquarters of the largest retailer in Arkansas, focused on developing strategy, plus two years in retail selling clothes to girls who were size zero, and two years recruiting high school students to study engineering
- Extracurricular involvement includes black belt in martial arts, volunteer ten-plus hours per week helping elementary school children.
- 25-year-old Asian-American female
- Goal: A career switch from engineering to social entrepreneurship

Odds of Success:

Harvard: 30%
Kellogg: 60%
MIT: -40%
Georgetown: 50%
UNC: 50%

Sandy's Analysis: OUCH! Lots to like here including K-Mart experience (aren't they the largest retailer in Arkansas?). By the way, show I saw about Wal-Mart said they hate MBAs and don't hire any and are proud of it. But, of course, you are not trying to get hired. You are trying to leave. This is just possibly an HBS profile, since Harvard likes the biggest anything, including biggest ***holes, of whom there are many in each section, and you have some other good karma working for you, including being an Asian Female in a Macho Company and how-you-overcame-that stories (I don't care if it is true or not, it is "truth-able," given what HBS and other schools think they know about Wal-Mart, so go with it).

Other good story ideas are dealing with anorexic fashion hounds and diverting them to therapy, recruiting high school kids, and volunteer work and black belt, which I take it, is not from Sam's Club? All that is great, and you might slip in, but the 3.4 GPA, even in an engineering program, and the 670, combined, might be your downfall. There is a saying, by me, that "HBS will blink once, but they will not blink twice," and you are asking them to blink at both your GPA and your GMAT, and they are reluctant to do that. Like everything else, it happens, but not all that often.

If you are hog wild about HBS, I'd keep taking the GMAT until you can't anymore. A 730 would really make a difference for you, and I do not say that to everyone about HBS. For the record, and for others reading this, if one has no HBS earmarks and a 690 GMAT, getting that score to 730 means zilch, so does getting that GMAT to 800. HBS is pretty GMAT agnostic past a certain point, it is only when GMAT and GPA are both on low side that raising your GMAT can help.

OK, back to K-Mart gal, you have a real solid shot at Kellogg, and should be very strong at GTown and UNC. MIT is more GMAT and GPA sensitive, especially in tandem, than most places, so I am calling that less than 40 percent. They also don't care so much about extras.

As to your goals about social entrepreneurship…huh? The best story you got going for you is having an engineering background and working for Wal-Mart. So why screw with that? Supply chain is the dirty secret of the Internet. Wal-Mart is the world's leader in supply chain. Sister, you've been given the royal touch at birth. Don't mess that up now and say you want to be a communist.

Say you're really interested in supply chain management, especially in stores, which cater to size zero people because the clothing often gets lost because it is so small. Well, just kidding, but you get the idea, some supply chain, retail operations leadership shtick.

Ms. Sassy

- 700 GMAT (Shooting for 700 but "standardized tests have historically not been my thing.")
- 3.3 GPA (I was young and slightly depressed)
- Undergraduate degree in chemical engineering from the number one public university in the U.S. and California
- Work experience includes three years managing over $3 million projects in product supply for the world's largest FMCG company. Now taking a break to work as a volunteer with an oil company corporate social responsibility initiative in the Niger Delta and hoping to not get kidnapped.
- Expect to return to employer and move to more early stage engineering work and contribute to company's expansion plans in Africa
- Extracurricular involvement teaching first-gen, low-income high school students how chemistry is used in the real world, outreach manager for AA theme house
- Why B-school? "I am tired of Africa being referred to as the dark continent and feel like the best way to do something tangible is to help Africans make money on a very large scale. Ultimately I want to help engineer joint ventures between governments, non-profits and for-profit enterprises that will run large high profit margin businesses – think clothes, beauty care etc. The end goal of this is to build human capital in Africa, create jobs and sustainable socio economic development."
- Concerns: "I suck at interviews – I have no filter!"
- 23-year-old sassy black female with "requisite tales of overcoming adversity – plane crashes, motherless babies, civil unrest, bombings, car crashes, jobless parents. I wish I were kidding but I'm not."

> **Odds of Success:**
>
> Harvard: 20%
> Stanford: 15%
> Sloan: 25%
> Tuck: 25%
> Yale: 30%+
> Cornell: 50%+

Sandy's Analysis: Are you a U.S. citizen? This is really important from a school's point of view because if not, you are African, which is nice. But if you are a U.S. citizen, you are African-American, which is an officially recognized and counted minority.

Now that we got that out of the way: you got a real solid story, which as you note needs to be edited, for PC reasons and just to get it straight.

Immigrant engineer, overcame adversity, worked for FMCG giant (for our readers who are baffled, that is <u>Fast Moving Consumer Goods</u>, and major players include Procter & Gamble, Kraft, Unilever, Nestle, and Coca Cola) both as an engineer and now during a sabbatical as a volunteer in Africa.

I am not sure if you left first job and volunteered for the Oil Company, or were sent there by first job. It's real important to make that clear and explain. Goals are, once again, some clear, and standardized version of what you got above, to wit, being an impactful leader in Africa, could take the form of doing 1 or 2. I admire X and Y and want to use those companies or those people as a role model.

Schools might blink at the 3.3 given engineering background and problems getting oriented to U.S. higher education, especially if high school was sub-par. As noted, schools do not like to blink twice, so GMAT becomes a bit more important for you. It would be worth really investing some time in that, both taking prep courses, and planning to take it more than once.

Just get a 680 if you can. Applicants with stories like yours sometimes get into HBS and Stanford, but usually with one or two boffo accomplishments beyond just doing well at work or with some big shot pushing you. For example, someone in Corporate Social Responsibility at the oil company you are now with who has contacts at those schools who can say, "This gal is really special."

You might get in based on story alone, but that is going to be iffy. Sloan does not go for do-gooders with low GPAs and GMATs, but they are always on the look out for minority women (assuming you are a U.S. citizen, they care, but less, about International Minority Women. Sloan does not seem your kind of place anyway, and you might think Chicago or Wharton or Columbia, where chances might be better and the MBA brand is just as good.

As to not interviewing well, dunno, a lot of that is getting your story straight and internalizing it. If you can put up with kidnappers in Niger, you should be able to deal with a 30-minute interview, although I realize the skill set is nominally different. My guess is, your interviewing problems are just based on not installing the right filters, not so much producing the words or thoughts.

Filtering is something that can be learned. Being a "sassy black female" is great on paper, less so if you are half sassy and half trying to be something different in an interview. Try being a focused and passionate black female instead.

98

Mr. Catholic

- 710 GMAT (Retake?)
- 3.97 GPA
- Undergraduate degree in finance & economics from a regionally ranked Midwestern Jesuit school ("I don't know whether this is significant or not, but all of my schooling (from pre-school through college) has been at Catholic institutions, and I can't deny the influence that my faith has had on my education.")
- Work experience includes a year as a finance systems analyst at a large, private consumer good manufacturer. Plan to remain at company for another three years and then head to B-school
- Extracurricular involvement as vice president of the largest fraternity on campus, a finance & econ tutor, volunteer work painting murals and mentoring elementary school children; various involvement at my neighborhood Catholic parish.
- First in family to go to college
- Goal: "I want to use the MBA to transition into management consulting with my overarching goal in life being to help as many American companies as possible to be successful and profitable (and beneficial to the American public) in an increasingly global and competitive economy (I know that sounds canned, but its the truth). I would particularly like to focus on making American manufacturing companies more nimble."
- 23-year-old Caucasian male from the Midwest, applying to Harvard and Wharton just for grins

---

Odds of Success:

Harvard: 20% to 30%
Wharton: 30% to 40%
Tuck: 40%+
Booth: 40%+
Texas: 50%+
Duke: 50%+

Sandy's Analysis: Business schools have nothing against Catholics or any other religion, and, in fact, like most people, have warm feelings about the focus and intensity of Jesuits (Pope's marines, etc, B-schools like Uncle Sam's Marines as well).

So there is no need to hide that. Also, first in your family to go to college is often a plus as well. What you need to do, though, is stop acting like a mild hick. That, they do not like.

You have a totally standard background, with a 3.97 from a regional college, a 710 GMAT and X years of work experience at a large, privately owned company. You don't need to apply to H/W just for 'grins' those schools take variants of kids like you all the time. A lot will turn on extras, recommendations, and not blowing interview.

Your goals are fine, but no need to giggle through them [viz, "my overarching goal in life being to help as many American companies as possible to be successful and profitable (and beneficial to the American public) in an increasingly global and competitive economy (I know that sounds canned, but its the truth). I would particularly like to focus on making American manufacturing companies more nimble"].

Just say that you interested in being an innovative and impactful leader in the manufacturing sector, and want to use technology and best management practices to make companies more nimble, sustainable, and competitive. It's just a matter of getting comfortable with business lingo like that, and being serious about it.

The best thing you can between now and when you apply is 1. Continue to do well at work, and try to get increasing leadership roles, 2. Build out some signature extracurricular involvement. It's okay to involve Church-based groups. B-schools like institutions of all kinds and the Catholic Church is famously the oldest institution in the world.

Ms. Environmental Engineer

- 690 GMAT (Retaking it)
- 3.6 GPA
- Undergraduate degree in environmental engineering from a university in India
- 3.6 Graduate GPA
- Master's degree in environmental engineering from Johns Hopkins University
- Work experience includes four years as an environmental engineer with one of the top consulting firms in the field; worked on a wide variety of projects related to water supply, water treatment, river and bridge systems
- Extracurricular involvement as a volunteer with terminally ill patients; also ran my first marathon this year and raised money for charities doing development work in India
- Goal: "Want to get into strategy and financing for environmental projects; In the long term, I see myself heading environmental infrastructure projects in developing countries"
- 26-year-old female born and raised in India

Odds of Success:

Harvard: 20% to 35%
Stanford: 15% to 20%
Wharton: 30% to 40%
Yale: 50%+
Berkeley: 50%+

Sandy's Analysis: Sounds good to me. Get a 700+ GMAT and a lot of this will turn on how well known your company is. You are similar to guys who work for oil companies, many of whom have comparable backgrounds

(Indian degree and US masters). They work all over the world, have lots of interesting experiences, and often get involved in extras related to their firms.

The difference is, there is no Exxon-Mobil of water—so that becomes important. Has anyone from your company applied to B-school? That could help, if schools know the company. Being a woman in this business is also a plus. Spend some time on essays dealing with how hard it is to gain authority with males at all levels in the infrastructure biz, which includes execs, field managers, and what I imagine are lots of hourly-wage worker types.

Volunteer work with the terminally ill is always a plus. Undergrad extra-currics count, so don't throw those away. You got an outside chance at HBS, Wharton and Stanford. Your GMAT becomes more important than usual, as it is with the oil guys. Try to get over 700.

"In the long term, I see myself heading environmental infrastructure projects in developing countries . . ." BINGO.

Mr. Blue Chip

- 570 GMAT (practice exam)
- 3.9 GPA
- Undergraduate degree in economics from a no-name state school
- Work experience includes two and one-half years in a finance/accounting job at a major blue chip company and then a leap to another blue chip high on the Fortune list in a job with greater responsibility
- Extracurricular involvement includes various volunteering activities.
- "I do have some good leadership experience, but some of it is politically charged and highly controversial and I'm not sure whether I should risk mentioning it."
- Career Goals: Upper management role in a blue chip firm. "My real goal is entrepreneurship and I have some action there, but if B-Schools despise entrepreneurs who "think big" and may, as a result, become "rich," then I guess people will be incentivized to hide that aspect of their personalities."
- Plan to matriculate at age 27 or 28. I would feel more ready if I could matriculate at 28, but I'm worried about age
- First in family to go to college from an extremely poor background

---

Odds of Success:

Harvard: 25%+
Stanford: 20%+
Wharton: 25%+
MIT Sloan: 20%
Chicago Booth: 40%+

Sandy's Analysis: Get the chip of your shoulder about schools disliking success and entrepreneurs and stop being paranoid about "politically charged" volunteer work, assuming it is not anti-gay rights, anti-choice (closer one, but downplay) or anti-immigrant. Dunno what I'd say if you were Tea Party honcho. That could be close and require special treatment. I probably would not mention Tea Party by name but just say you are an activist for limited government.

On the bright side, you got a lot going for you, including a 3.9 at a non-name school, poverty, first in family to go to college and a couple of blue chip jobs. High GPA from a no-where school and Blue Chip work experience is usually a great formula to get into top schools. Just try to get some kinda 650 GMAT.

The fact that you got 3.9 as Econ major will go a long way in giving schools assurance that you can hack B-school math. As to goals: YES, stick with wanting to be a leader in a Blue Chip firm and do not, out of the blue, say you want to be an entrepreneur. That does just not compute and anyone can say that. You could also say, in the proper application lingo, that you want to lead a 'growing' or 'innovative' firm or make some Blue Chip firm more so.

I don't think it makes a big difference if you matriculate at 27 or 28, although 27 is probably better. But if you say you want to be a management consultant or join some Fortune 100 leadership program after earning your MBA, most schools will see that as plausible even if you are 31 at graduation.

Guys like you, with real victim and sob stories and full backing of firm, get into Stanford with a ~700 GMAT. HBS takes dudes like you, if you execute properly. MIT cares the least for sob stories, and the GMAT really counts over there, so chances are the least there, oddly. Wharton would like a 680. Best chance with a 650 would be HBS, strange to say. You don't need to push any envelopes on the application, just take a regular-sized envelope and address it very clearly.

Mr. Frat Boy

- 750 GMAT
- 3.7 GPA
- Undergraduate degree from Iowa State in engineering with a business specialization
- Work experience includes two years with Samsung in a purchasing/supply chain management role
- Extracurricular involvement as leader in a college fraternity, leader of a 200+ member employee group at work, leader for local American Cancer Society, leader in mentoring program for disadvantaged youth
- Fluent in Mandarin and working now on Portuguese
- 23-year-old "non-academic minority" male

Odds of Success

Harvard: 50+%
Stanford: 40+%
Wharton: 60%
MIT: 60+%
Kellogg: 60+%
Chicago: 60+%
Duke: 70+%

Sandy's Analysis: I don't know what "non-academic minority" male means, honestly, and if the rest of your application is that screwed up, you can shoot yourself in the foot next to your non-foot.

Otherwise, this is pretty clear-cut. Guys from brand-name companies with three years of work experience in some boring, but important role like purchasing and supply chain, and who also have a 3.7 GPA in an engineering program from yes, even Iowa State with a 750 GMAT, and what sounds like solid and powerful extras, well, guys like you get into H/S/W depending on not screwing up, a bit of luck, serviceable (not brilliant just okay) execution of an application, solid recommendations and a bit more luck, but not much.

You are totally solid on paper, although given what I detect is some chip on your shoulder, you might screw yourself in person, or have that chip on your shoulder emerge in essays, but maybe I exaggerate, and you're just regular corn-fed Big Ten "non-academic minority" male who got carried away in your note to us.

We forgive you, but don't get carried away in application execution. Stanford will depend on crafting some "identity politics" story (if you know what that means), and you never know there, but HBS takes guys like you left and right, and so does Wharton. Other places should be slam dunks if you convince them you want to come.

Mr. Unemployed

- 710 GMAT
- 2.94 GPA
- Undergraduate degree in engineering from a big state school
- Work experience includes three years of entry-level work, but unemployed for two years "due to economy and poor credit"
- "I will have mediocre recommendations since I haven't really had major responsibilities in my entry level jobs"

Odds of Success:

Wharton: Zero
Columbia: Zero
Cornell: Zero
UCLA: Zero
Boston University: -20%
Arizona State: -30%
Baruch: 30%

Sandy's Analysis: I feel your pain, pal, but schools won't. You are not getting into any top-15 business school with this profile. There is just no compelling reason to take you. Business schools are not in the business of getting jobs for unemployed people. They are in the business of taking wonderfully employed people and making sure they stay that way. Your explaining to them how the MBA will help you excel in the future is the last thing they want to hear. They don't go for the Lourdes routine.

You don't enter Harvard, Stanford or Wharton and then throw away your crutches. You enter H/S/W on a motorcycle and leave in a Ferrari.

You really need to look into some regional schools, or night programs. The 710 will go a long way there–although even there, try to present a concrete future plan, based on prior work, and not some miracle story. Sorry to be even a bit flip. I hope things turn around for you.

Mr. Rugby

- 700 GMAT
- 3.8 Grade Point Average
- Undergraduate degree in chemical engineering from Texas Tech University
- Work resume includes Shell Oil internship, Eastman Chemical Co-op, TETRA Technologies internship though "college senior"
- Extracurricular involvement includes All-State player and fundraising chair in men's rugby, servant leader in Christ in Action, and more
- Goal to develop long-term assisted living centers
- 22-year-old Nigerian American "fresh out of college"
- "I am neither a button-pusher or a rough-neck but more like a combo of both."

Odds of Success:

Harvard Business School 2+2 Program: 40% to 55%
MIT joint MS in Engineering with MBA: 60%
Kellogg MBA or MMM: 60%
Wharton: 60%
Columbia: 60+%
Darden: 70%
Duke: 70%
Michigan: 70+%
Carnegie Mellon: 70+%

Sandy's Analysis: I am assuming you are a college senior and an American citizen, although your note says "22-year-old Nigerian American (fresh out of college)" and that is unclear and you also say "college senior" in another part of your story.

Anyway, if you are an African-American, e.g. a U.S citizen, with a 3.8 in chemical engineering from an ok school, and a 700 GMAT, with some blue-chip job intern experience, and you can max out your extra curricular stuff, which seems strong, and drop your out-of-no-place idea to "develop assisted living centers" (WTF!!!!) and stay in the energy business somehow, you got a lot to like.

HBS 2+2 program takes kids like you if you can execute without pissing them off, a small IF given note above (both tone deaf and confusing in its original form, which claimed profiles were getting boring, although the snarky parts were omitted by John, our resident diplomat), and you seem to have some solid extras, plus that 3.8 GPA. They will blink at the 700, if the 3.8 is legit and not some mash up of your favorite courses. The same goes for HBS if in fact you are out of college, as you also say you are, or is 'fresh out of college' your short term goal.

If you, or anyone else, is applying during their first year of work experience, HBS might accept you and defer you. MIT is always looking for African Americans with 700 GMATs not to mention 3.8 in chemical engineering. MIT has a minority problem, in part because they used to be stingy with scholarships, for everyone, but that might have changed. Stanford goes for kids like you, if you can put together some interesting identity politics story, based on your background and extras. Wharton is always looking for 3.8 GPA/700 GMAT black males as well. Other schools should be solid if you can convince them you want to attend.

Mr. Valedictorian

- 750 GMAT
- 4.0 GPA
- Undergraduate degree in science with first class honors and valedictorian at Kenyan University
- 3.0 Graduate GPA
- Master's in medicine and surgery
- Founded a company and grew it to more than 80 clients in two years
- Extracurricular involvement as student leader in HIV/AIDS advocacy group
- "Would like to get into healthcare venture capital for the developing markets"

Odds of Success:

Harvard Business School: 10%
Stanford: 10%
Wharton: -20%
Columbia: -20%
Kellogg: -30%
Cornell: 30%

Sandy's Analysis: Dunno, need more info, and I may not fully understand your graduate degree? Is that a medical degree? Are you eligible to get certified to practice medicine in the U.S.? Have you ever practiced medicine? What kind of company did you found? And why, given apparent success, are you putting it on hiatus to attend MBA program.

Getting into venture capital in most cases requires prior experience in banking or VC itself, although sometimes a VC shop will make an exception for subject matter expert, and yes, doctors, which is why I ask.

Age?

Well, let's start with the good stuff, 750 and the 4.0. That is great but what we expect to see next is some selective and classy job at a government agency or consulting company or, after your Bachelor of Medicine degree some alliance with an institution that business schools have experience with.

Lacking that, you really need to explain the reasons why you started a company and what it does. Schools are very skeptical of African credentials as a hangover from a raft of scandals involving false transcripts and invalidated standardized tests. I don't have a handle on the current state of this, but I do know that makes it doubly important for African candidates to have established jobs, since the schools think the employers on the ground are best able to filter out credential irregularities in the first instance.

Without that, I am not seeing this as an HBS, Stanford, or Wharton admit unless you can convince them of bona fides of schooling, work, etc. and decision making processes. Other schools may require the same. That is a gateway issue for you. It just could be that your post was too terse on details. If so, pay attention to what I note above and adjust accordingly.

Mr. Ivy League

- 700 GMAT
- 3.8 GPA
- Undergraduate degree from a Harvard/Yale/Princeton Ivy in 2007
- Worked in private equity in New York for two years and two-plus years for a venture capital fund in Vietnam run by HBS grads
- Extracurriculars include playing a division one sport for four years, managing a softball team in a local international softball league, various alumni association work and random charity work

---

Odds of Success:

Harvard Business School: 40% to 70%
Stanford: 30% to 55%
Wharton: 50% to 80%
Chicago: 60% to 90% (just convince Booth you want to come)

Sandy's Analysis: Man (and I am assuming you are a man), this sounds pretty solid and interesting. Guys like you get into Harvard and Stanford depending on execution, recommendations, luck, and at HBS, not blowing the interview.

You are anchored by a 3.8 GPA and a D1 sport, which they respect, especially if it was a team sport, viz. football, baseball, basketball, and their absolute favorite, crew. I don't know why crew is such a favorite, maybe it is because Adcoms are gals, and have gauzy mental pictures of hunks on the water, or maybe because the historical record of crew guys at HBS is pretty thick, although women's crew also a plus and surprisingly the crew admits are often coxswains (low weight Asian gals with big mouths, or regular mouths which feel very comfy around a megaphone, which I believe the team provides).

The one soft spot is the GMAT, but they will blink at that, in light of high GPA, solid splits (81/89) and just an interesting story. Some issues would be, as always, what is the record of your employer sending kids to H/S/W and do those HBS grads running the Vietnam fund have any beyond-ordinary pull.

You will need to be very strategic about presenting your extra-currics because they seem wide rather than deep. That is okay, and it is often preferred. Kids with deep involvement in one thing often get overwhelmed trying to present it, while other kids, who ran one fundraiser, really dig deep and capture in granular detail the various ways they were effective, which oddly (and unfairly) often comes off better than the major player's confusing essay. Just use some of those extras, especially recent ones, as accomplishments or setbacks, capture a team story, a couple of work stories, and some blah blah goal statement about how PE can transform Asia. Add some jive about how X business school can help you, and you could be a winner, especially at Harvard and Wharton.

Stanford gets a bunch of guys like you, and takes some, so a lot there will turn on being winning and Stanfordy in app and essays. What is Stanfordy? It is someone Derrick Bolton (director of admissions) takes a shine to, after you have passed the velvet rope of GPA/GMAT/employment test that gets you inside the club. Then Derrick has to like your personal story, attitude, and values.

Wharton might balk at the GMAT. They seem very touchy about that recently, but jeepers, their average is 718 and someone has to be below that. Why not you?

Mr. Operations

- 780 GMAT
- 3.71 GPA
- Undergraduate degree in industrial engineering from the Georgia Institute of Technology
- Work experience as a manufacturing engineer at a top-heavy construction machinery maker in the Midwest
- Extracurriculars include teaching English and interview coaching with local Hispanic population. Involved in local theatre company with lead roles in several performances.
- 24 years old
- Latino-American

Odds of Success:

Harvard Business School: 50% to 60%
Stanford: 50% to 60%
Wharton: 60% to 70%
Kellogg: 60% to 70%
Columbia: 60% to 70%

Sandy's Analysis: Seems to be the Trifecta and more: 1. Minority, 2. Jumbo GMAT, 3. Solid GPA from an iconic school, and 4. You even work at a place that actually makes stuff. Guys like you should get into Harvard, Stanford or Wharton so long as there is no-damaging execution, in other words, just don't screw it up. Schools really are on the look out, they say, for manufacturing types, and assuming the Latino deal is solid, in terms of actual influence and even name and activities versus having some great grand mom from Cuba hidden in your family tree, well yeah, this is all good.

Make sure those clowns at the factory can write the usual exaggerated recommendations (sometimes factory types in the Mid-West suffer from this affliction called telling the truth, a real danger for a recommendation writer. Just show them this handy dandy recommendation converter:

Translation: "Outstanding" equals average. "Best person I have ever seen" equals will lead the free world based on his impact here and that is not only my opinion but also our CEO, who will be calling you.

And don't blow the interview at HBS. You can blow it at Stanford. They will enjoy taking you and frosting the alum who dared to say your motives for going to Stanford seemed murky and your teamwork answers were ego-centric. As if Derrick Bolton cares about egocentricity when you got a 780.

Mr. Internet Startup

- 720 GMAT
- 3.8 GPA
- Earned a joint BS/MA degree in applied economics from a 50ish ranked private university
- 26 years old
- Built, launched and ran a web startup that ultimately failed
- Writing has been published by The New York Times
- International traveler who is also a self-taught computer programmer
- Extracurriculars include volunteer experience and soccer and rugby player

> **Odds of Success:**
>
> Harvard Business School: Less than 30%
> Stanford: Less than 30%
> Wharton: 40%
> MIT Sloan: 50%
> Dartmouth: 50%
> Columbia: 60% if early admission

Sandy's Analysis: You are a good example of a guy with a lot of impressive stuff that weighs more in the real world than it does on planet admissions (which is sorta like the moon in some cases, with its own gravity field). A 3.8 GPA and a 720 GMAT are totally fine, as is quant background. Spending four years with a web startup is something schools will pay lip service to, but at bottom, they would prefer that you either worked for Google or founded Groupon, never got an MBA, and gave them a building in 30 years. There is not much in between. Ditto on your writing published in The New York Times. I am impressed but schools don't care all that much since it does fit in their wheelhouse. (And the record of journos who do attend business school is mixed: they often write tell-alls, which have been done already).

Why do you want an MBA? That will be key. This ain't smelling like a H/S/W admit, although maybe Wharton. You should try Sloan, which nominally says they like entrepreneurs. I have my doubts about how many kids they admit with only entrepreneurship experience (Rod Garcia–the MIT Adcom head—if you are reading this, please check in and tell us).

The trouble with you from the school's POV is that you are too self-taught and that seems to be your preferred model. You need to explain why you need an MBA and MBA training. This is like that Eagles song <u>Desperado</u>. That has been your M.O. and now it is time to explain why you have come to your senses.

Ahem…

Desperado, why don't you come to your senses?

You been out ridin' fences for so long now.

Oh, you're a hard one

I know that you got your reasons

These things that are pleasin' you

Can hurt you somehow

Ms. Engineer

- 760 GMAT
- 3.5 GPA
- Undergraduate degree in mechanical engineering from MIT
- Work experience includes five years at Hewlett Packard as an R&D engineer
- Extracurricular involvement in a company employee resource group, including two years as chairperson; set up networking events, executive speaker series; also four years as a 50-to-100-hour-a-year volunteer at a girls science and technology program
- Goal: To move into product management in high tech
- 26-year-old female

> **Odds of Success:**
>
> Stanford: 30%
> MIT: 40+%
> Northwestern: 50+%
> Berkeley: 50+%
> Duke: 50+%

Sandy's Analysis: Is that 3.5 at MIT on a 4 or 5 scale? That's really key. Assuming it is 3.5/4 well, come on down. We got a female with good grades at MIT in a bona fide science major, a premium GMAT score, 760, and five years (well, maybe one or two too many) at HP, which is still a respected company – although not by me (as a longtime – real long – stockholder and former ink junkie for your printers before I went back to toner and a generic printer which never jams or needs ink). Plus you have a ton of good service work in your company and impactful volunteer work with science and girls, a hot button issue.

Why are you not including HBS and Wharton in your picks? Didn't "Dee" Leopold in her Wall Street Journal interview say they are looking for engineers? While that may not be true, e.g. that they are looking, well, they will certainly be open to one who shows up at their door, especially one wearing a dress, or who could wear a dress without attracting too many double takes. Wharton will be very favorable on stats alone.

If GPA is 3.5/5, well, you still got a chance, although that is a negative obviously, but with a 760 GMAT and a MIT degree, you got a lot going for you. I would think higher than Product Manager in stating my goals. In reality, product manager is a super big deal, but within the fever-swamp of an admissions office, it sounds like Death of Salesman stuff, some poor schmuck with a sample bag and a broken down Buick.

You need to say you want to be a leader in new areas of technology. Stanford might be a reach, if there is nothing driving you, unless you have some spit on the ball there by way of connections at HP, or can really play up your great extra of working with the Girls and Technology club. At HBS, they take kids like you with just serviceable execution and some luck and strong recs. At MIT, a lot may depend on real GPA and how well you fit their innovation mantra. But as noted before, they don't kiss off too many 760 GMATs from applicants with clean criminal records (unless you are otherwise ultra nerdy, which is saying something over there). Haas and Duke should be slam dunks if you can convince them you want to come.

Ms. Software Management

- 700 GMAT
- 3.9 GPA
- Undergraduate degree in molecular and cellular biology from a top 20 university
- Work experience includes four-plus years in first sales and marketing and now software product management for a renewable energy company
- Extracurricular involvement as president of an organization that ran freshman orientation at my college, held offices in sorority, volunteered for a nonprofit that aspires to do solar energy in developing countries
- Goal: "To repeat the success of my current company but in the developing world" in a for-profit model
- Why MBA? "I've witnessed one highly successful example in the corporate world but a broad business education would really accelerate my professional development. A school with a strong entrepreneurial focus is a must."
- 27-year-old female

> **Odds of Success:**
>
> Stanford: 20% to 30%
> Harvard: 30% to 40%
> Berkeley: 50+%
> MIT: 40% to 50+%

Sandy's Analysis: Hmmm, a 3.9 in molecular biology and a 700 GMAT plus 4.5 years of solid work in what appears to be an exciting and successful start-up—and a woman? That could make most schools wink at the low Q score on your GMAT. And added course work is another plus. The fact that you'll be 28 year old and have six years of work experience when you go to school is on the high side for Harvard and Stanford, but they maybe they will wink at that, too.

Not sure what first job was, or if you have had one job or two—sounds like two and first job could be important as just some filter of what you did right out of college. All that said, you are on the bubble for a place like HBS and Stanford. They take and ding people like you, depending on execution, recommendations, luck, and luck, and not blowing the interview. Execution will count a bit more in your case, since you don't have a full blue chip background. But if your current company is a leader in its field, stress that.

Also make the most of your non-profit work for solar in developing countries since that links with your goals. As to goals per se, you say, "deploying renewal energy in developing world with a for-profit model." That is probably OK, though pointing to some companies who have done that would help. Since you work for a successful version of that model, that is also strong evidence of your bona fides.

You say, "A school with a strong entrepreneurial focus is a must"—kiddo, today that is every school. My advice to you and everyone: Go to the best school you get into. 'Focus' is pretty meaningless–both for your experience and for employers. Sure on the margin, if you are interested in banking, maybe Tuck is good at that, and has connections, but as a rule, applicants should just attend the best school they can get into.

If you had to pick between HBS and Stanford with this story, well, maybe Stanford is more up your alley since a lot of renewable activity is in California. But I would not choose Berkeley over HBS for that reason.

Mr. Oil Driller

- 690 GMAT (will retake)
- 3.3 GPA
- Undergraduate degree in mechanical engineering from the University of Mumbai
- Work experience as a project leader with Halliburton Offshore Services for the past 16 months, managing a group of up to ten people, and for the prior ten months with ITS Energy Services, another oil field company, where he had been promoted to sales engineer
- Extracurricular involvement as a member of my university's cricket team, president of the engineering students' association, leader of several college festivals, participant in intercollegiate quizzes and fashion shows
- 25-year-old male

Odds of Success:

Harvard: 10%
Dartmouth: 20% to 30%
Duke: 20% to 50%
Michigan: 20% to 50%
Yale: 20% to 40%
Texas: 50+%
Virginia: 50+%
ISB: 30+%

Sandy's Analysis: Oil and gas guys are the same black box to B-school adcoms as the military – and that includes guys working for the majors such as Shell and Exxon/Mobil or the service companies such as Halliburton and Schlumberger. Adcoms have very little idea what you actually do (assuming you are not in corporate development in the home office). Everyone has stories about working on rigs with lots of people from different countries, many of whom are low-paid laborers, and dealing with emergencies, cultural diversity, and alleged marvels of increased production brought about by your hands-on expertise.

Thus, very often, like the military, issues like GPA and GMAT and even extras, schooling and pedigree of any kind really count since you actual experience gets homogenized. The oil and gas Desis who get into Harvard Business School frequently went to IIT or other top Indian schools and have real high GPA and GMATs as well as some X factor like super-duper recommendations from someone who can write one, or powerful extras, or just 10% less than that and some luck. You are off that model by more than 10% since you got a lower GPA, started at a non-blue chip company, ITS Energy Services (well, seems non-blue chip to me, I'm no expert and I hope I am not insulting anyone), seemed to have changed jobs rather quickly, and extras like quizzing and fashion are not impactful in this game.

I realize quizzing is a big deal in India, but adcoms don't get it. And if they do, they merely view it like intramural athletics: something you do for yourself and not others. Also, as you perceive, the 690 GMAT is not helping you fight above your weight, either. I'm not sure how Mumbai U stacks up in the Indian school hierarchy, but it is not IIT. So I ain't seeing this as HBS.

At other schools you note, this begins to look a lot better because Halliburton is a well-known company, your GPA and GMAT numbers begin to fall into their range, and hey, it looks like you will get a job back in the energy patch when you graduate, given your background. All that puts you in the running there. Get a 730 GMAT and get lucky, and you could maybe slip into Wharton, even though you did not ask.

Mr. Family Business

- 730 GMAT
- 3.75 GPA
- Undergraduate degree in chemical engineering from an "average state school"
- Work experience includes time at NASA after school, though I currently sit second in command at my family's privately owned, $50 million (sales) business
- Goal: "Eventually I'll be taking over this organization and I want to go to business school to help support that transition. I am local to Massachusetts so I'd prefer HBS or Sloan."
- "Have a couple of friends who are recent graduates from both programs who are willing to write alumni recommendations."

> **Odds of Success:**
>
> Harvard: 20% to 35+%
> MIT: 40% to 50+%

Sandy's Analysis: Running a family business is a double-edged sword for adcoms. HBS sees itself as creating a transforming experience (they don't keep data on this, which makes their belief in this aspiration even more tenacious) and they can quietly gag on the idea of having some guy who is near-running a family business go back there. All that said, there is some unspoken number about the size of a family business, which turns it from a liability to an asset in the eyes of the HBS adcom. MIT is less picky about seeing family businesses as 'non-transformational' experiences but that lurks in the background there as well.

I don't know what that number is. My guess is, though, it is more than $50 million a year in sales. Another issue is how 'hip' the business is from adcom's point of view. If you are running some alt-energy business or cutting-edge medical device company or educational technology company which could be expanded into some BIG DEAL under your stewardship, and not only expanded but also transformed into an enterprise that is more meaningful and impactful while also becoming a hiring magnet to boot (of handicapped, minority, and immigrant labor at excellent wages) –well, that is a dreamscape that sometimes works at HBS. So my advice is, whatever your business is in reality, try to make your plans for it align with that vision.

MIT might go for the 730, 3.75 and NASA triple play (plus background in chemical engineering). The added attraction for any school is that they don't have to find you a job. HBS might go for some of that, but it may take more–make it real clear why you need an MBA in the first place, and really think hard about creating a snow globe of a picture of what you are going to do with Dad's company.

As to your point of having recent grads write recommendations, that does not cut a whole lot of mustard at either school unless the grads are friendly with adcom officials or are recent donor grads, and not $100 to the class fund. What you need are recommendations from customers, bankers or investors who can confirm your potential to create the wonderful picture you paint about the transformed business.

Mr. Insecure Engineer

- 790 GMAT
- 3.76 GPA
- Undergraduate degree in management and electrical engineering from the University of Pennsylvania
- Work experience includes two years at a Big 3 consulting firm
- Extracurricular involvement as president of the dean's advisory board in college, leader of the school's chemical engineering club and a volunteer tutor for children in West Philadelphia. I've also done volunteer consulting work for non-profits
- "I'm a little curious as to how schools will perceive my Wharton undergrad background. I'm afraid that it might make it substantially harder for me to answer the "Why do you want an MBA?" and the "What will you get out of an MBA?" questions. I'm nervous that b-schools will think I should just go to an engineering firm directly from consulting because I've already taken a lot of business classes."

Odds of Success:

Harvard: 40% to 50%
Stanford: 30+%
Wharton: 50+%
Dartmouth: 50+%
MIT: 50%
Chicago: 50+%

Sandy's Analysis: Dude, chill out. B-schools are not going to question why you want an MBA after doing a dual business and engineering degree at Wharton as an undergraduate. Saying you are interested in some intersection of business and engineering and having the cred to prove it, in terms of an electrical engineering degree, is gold. All you need to say is that you want to be an impactful leader like X, Y and Z and then find some guys who are powerful and progressive CEOs with engineering backgrounds. That should not be hard.

How not hard? <u>This guy</u>, at the National Engineers Week Foundation says, "According to a recent ranking by Business Week of CEOs of the top 1,000 publicly held U.S. companies, more chief executive officers majored in engineering - not marketing, not finance, and not law - than any other discipline." So just read that press release which names names (and which oddly does not have a full date attached, kinda like leaving an elevator out of a skyscraper, but I digress, and that is why that dude is writing press releases and not designing bridges).

The rest of your story is super solid, with Big 3 consulting experience. As for that 790 GMAT, some say that is better than an 800 since schools like to brag about how many 800 kids they ding (talking to you Derrick Bolton at Stanford!). For an interesting other anecdote about 790 versus 800, note that the chairman of the Stanford University Department of Statistics said that they consider the scores equal (on some super-duper math/stats test the require for admission) since there is not any statistical significance between the two scores, and, ahem, that is something they try to respect.

Guys like you get dinged at HBS if they blow the interview, which can happen for lots of reasons, and at Stanford if they get unlucky and hit a PC landmine. Being CEO of a company like G.E. or more smartly, being an impactful leader at a company like GE in order to make the world better is an acceptable goal statement. And saying that an MBA will help you become a better general manager, decision maker, investor, people-person is totally fine.

Ms. Doctor

- 770 GMAT
- 3.93 GPA
- Undergraduate degree in biochemistry and neurobiology from the University of Washington
- Work experience includes internship and research as I am a first year medical student at the University of Minnesota
- "I am looking for schools with MD/MBA joint programs and hope to get into one of the accelerated MBA programs."
- International student from China, fluent in Chinese and English

---

Odds of Success:

Harvard: 20%
Wharton: 30%
Chicago: 30%
Northwestern: 30%
Cornell: 40%
Columbia: 40%

Sandy's Analysis: Jeepers, I'm impressed. I think you'll get in someplace with those high stats, although you will need some jive as to why you want a joint degree. The usual suspects are Health Care Management (e.g. run a hospital or HMO) or pharma or medical device executive, or on occasion government service or some combination of the above.

A really hot field now is IT + medical records, since everyone thinks that better medical record technology is going to save everyone $$$$ and provide the basis for Medicine Ball (data rich protocols to optimize care, a la Money Ball, don't hold your breath.)

At HBS, they usually have about 12 docs or so, but those students are often from Harvard or Yale Medical School, and often have MD's already and then get the MBA, sometimes during residency or early training.

I'll be honest, I'm not sure of the logistics of joint degree programs. The best thing you can do is figure out what your GOAL for those programs would be, from the list above, and then head in the direction of that goal by choosing electives and jobs—that would really strengthen your chances and story.

Please take my predictions with one very big grain of salt because I don't know enough about joint degree programs. But if you do well in med school, and create some record, which leads to a joint-degree goal, I think you will be successful. Saying you want to help reform medical care delivery in China would be a BOFFO thing to say, but you would need some record of working in China or working with organizations which do that.

Mr. Biotech

- 750 – 800 Q GRE (waiting for final scaled score)
- 670 – 770 Verbal
- 3.9 GPA
- Undergraduate degree from University of North Carolina
- 4.0 masters GPA
- Graduate degree from UNC
- PhD in genetics
- Founded a biotech company, raising $2.6 million. Still operational, but not to revenue. Also founded a health-fitness focused IT company and am raising a first round in the first quarter of 2012. Expect to stay involved with company, albeit in a reduced role, through business school
- "B-school will make me a better leader, manager and allow me to grow the business faster by leveraging information and networks gained during MBA."
- "I'm applying with the new GRE scores. Haven't seen a single analysis done on a PhD-holding entrepreneur applicant using the GRE to apply.
- 30-year-old South Asian

Odds of Success:

Harvard: 30%
Stanford: 30%
MIT: 40% to 50+%
Duke: 50+%
UNC: 50+%

Sandy's Analysis: You ain't got a GRE issue, you got a WTF issue. WTF are you applying to B school for?

Your answer, "B-School will make me a better leader, manager and allow me to grow the business faster by leveraging information and networks gained during MBA."

Well, not that it matters, but the only part of that statement which is, in fact, true is that B-school may help you network. It will not make you a better leader or manager nor will it help you "leverage information" whatever that means.

All that being said, I can't think of any better reasons you could give, which goes to show, there ain't any real reasons. I don't know what your real story is, but if only 30 percent of the above is true in some meaningful way– e.g., your Biotech company is a 'real' Biotech company and that is not your way of saying you are selling cat urine extract on the internet to former coke addicts who want to think they are still doing cocaine (former addicts will understand this, something about doing coke smelled or tasted like cat urine, really, those were the days)–well, dunno. I just don't see the value to YOU, or more importantly, to any VC, in you getting an MBA.

But so what? If you are still interested, for whatever reasons, you need to make it clear that you are doing this not as a serial entrepreneur wash out but as someone who is just, well, sensational and crazy in a good way.

Will the schools see it this way? That is hard to predict. I think you are not getting into HBS or Stanford because they just don't need your high numbers and will ask the same questions I am asking. And if they get past that, they may wonder, correctly, if you will drop out, once you find out how boring the whole deal is. But allow me to hedge my bets in this way.

One thing you do have going is not what the school can do for you, but what you do for the school. That is potentially a lot, given that you appear to be one hell of an interesting entrepreneur with a lot of war stories and the added lottery ticket stub of possibly becoming a zillionaire if any of those companies work out. I do not overlook this.

MIT might bite because they sometimes fall for big numbers alone, and yours are real solid, and they might see some value in your being an actual example of what they claim they are trying to turn out anyway. Duke and UNC should admit you just to put you in the front window of their stats, visiting days, and brochures.

If you get blanked at MBA level, look into the Stanford-Sloan program, the one-year B.S. in business degree program, which operates out of both MIT and Stanford. If you went to the one at Stanford, you'd get a LOT of the networking value and save yourself a year. I know grads of this program. They had backgrounds sorta similar to yours, and they were happy campers. Go visit and check it out.

Mr. Poker Player

- 710 GMAT
- 2.7 GPA
- Undergraduate degree in biology from UC-San Diego
- "Played poker to support self through undergrad to pay for schooling, thus low grades"
- Work experience includes four years at a biotech company, having transitioned from R&D to business development
- Extracurricular involvement coaching Pop Warner football for four years, three years on non-profit research foundation for an incurable children's heart disease
- Goal: To use the MBA to get into a business development role in Big Pharma, then move back into leading my own BD group in biotech
- Chinese-American born in Shanghai, came to U.S. at age of 4

Odds of Success:

Harvard: -10%
Stanford: -10%
Wharton: -15%

Sandy's Analysis: The 2.7 is going to be hard to live down. I just don't see this happening at Harvard or Stanford with low GPA, so-so jobs, and no gold dust. Wharton is not likely either, to be frank. Guys like you go to Chicago or Kellogg on a long shot, and maybe schools that U.S. News would rank 8th to 15th where with this background, your dreams can come true anyway.

Your extras are good, but not going to tilt this in any meaningful way at H/S/W. Poker as reason for low grades will not cut much slack. An amazing number of applicants play Poker, some kids with stints as pros, and they often have good grades. How did you get hired as a "researcher" at a bio-tech firm with a 2.7? No offense, but scary. Aren't there a surplus of dudes with MA's and Ph.D's in bio?

I might change my mind if your biotech company is a "blue-chip" type shop and has a history of sending its business development people to top business schools.

The Consultants

Consultants make up a big chunk of the students in MBA programs. At Harvard and Wharton, slightly more than one in five incoming MBA candidates in 2011 came direct to campus from a consulting firm. At Stanford, some 17% of the entering class in the fall hailed from the field of consulting.

Outside of investment banking and investment management, the consulting industry is one of the few where an MBA degree is something of a rite of passage. At most of the elite consulting firms, you'd be hard-pressed to make partner without an MBA degree from an elite business school.

So there are plenty of consultants who apply. This section contains a fair cross section of applicants with consulting backgrounds. Not all of them are from the big three: McKinsey, Boston Consulting Group, and Bain & Co. Frankly, if you come from one of those three firms and have strong recommendations from a partner or two, you're petty much a shoo in to a prestige business school.

Far more interesting is what happens when you work for a second-tier firm or a boutique. You'll often notice that Sandy often asks applicants if the firms they work for have a record of sending candidates to a specific business school. If they do, the chances of an applicant rise considerably. If not, it becomes much more difficult.

Ms. Tiffany

- 760 GMAT
- 3.4 GPA
- Undergraduate degree in finance and accounting from the University of Virginia McIntire School of Commerce
- Study abroad program in Shanghai during third year
- Three years as a consultant at Accenture
- Extracurricular activities include being on the Board of Directors for a student-run UVA recruiting organization, an Alumni Trustee for McIntire, Junior League of Washington (non-profit women's volunteer organization), various lead positions for groups within Accenture (Women's Networking Group, Consultant Action Team)
- Goal is to pursue a career change from management consulting to strategy and marketing for a luxury retail company

---

Odds of Success:

Wharton: 35% to 45%
Columbia: 35% to 50%
New York University: 50+%
Virginia: 50% to 70%
Duke: 50% to 70%

Sandy's Analysis: Well, you already got a Tiffany GMAT score so your luxury marketing career can start with yourself. Lots to like, and this just reads like a hi-performing networking, clubby, clear story about a gal who went to UVA, stopped partying enough to major in Finance and Accounting, and got a gig at Accenture, which is solid.

Schools like Alum Trustees as well, for obvious reasons, including the high 'satisfaction' scores they give the school on BusinessWeek surveys. The 3.4 GPA is the small stain on this otherwise beautiful table set for two (you and the school) and the issue is, how glaring that will be amid all the candlelight and mood music.

Duke and UVA will go for this 3.4 and all, you are deeply their type, and 3.4 is kinda their average GPA.

Ditto NYU. Columbia may have trouble not staring at your 760, and since its average GPA is only 3.5, I'd say you got a real good shot there, too. Wharton has been known to ogle a 760 as well, and as noted, the rest of your story is attractive to any school. Trouble is, Wharton sees big numbers all the time, although so do I, and I still look. I was actually surprised—when I just looked it up—to note that the average GPA at Wharton is 3.5. That leaves us with the Accenture issue, a consulting firm, which places kids into all B-schools but just not as many kids as McKinsey, Bain, and BCG.

Makes this something of a coin toss there. A good deal may ride on how high-performing you are at Accenture in terms of getting great recommendations which say what an ace you are, how fast you got promoted or what stories you can come up about high-profile projects.

As to your stated goal of marketing for a luxury retail company, let me suggest that sounds like wanting to marry a great husband and move to Connecticut like Mad Men's Betty Draper. Especially if none of your consulting work has been similar. Why not just say you want to transition into boutique consulting for retail companies or lead a retail department of a major consulting company? What do you think adding the word luxury is getting you? Stay with consulting and retail, and present yourself as excited by all kinds of retail, including electronics, yadda, yadda, yadda.

There are lots of challenges for retail consultants finding a new audience and new "platforms," something you cannot say about luxury retail marketing, unless you count platform shoes. Retail consulting has lots of data crunching (you hear that Wharton?). And hey, you have already been a consultant, and will not have a hard time getting a job. If you are sick of consulting, a vibe I am getting somehow, well, just hold your nose and say what I told you. You won't be the first.

Ms. Education

- 690 GMAT (Looking to retake to score around target school average or above 720+)
- 3.4 GPA
- Undergraduate degree in public policy from a top 10 national private university
- Work experience as a portfolio manager/senior consultant at an educational technology consulting firm in a very niche sector, international client base.
- Promoted twice in 3 years, youngest in role by 5 to 10 years, manage one of largest portfolios both in terms of revenue and client size.
- Presented at national and international conferences/workshops and launched online professional learning community.
- Extracurricular activities in college with leadership positions, selective women's leadership program, community tutoring, sorority executive board, led campus faith organization, education policy internship and organized passing of landmark educational bill.
- Goal: To start my own educational consulting firm/start up or lead an educational organization/school/district, short term: non-profit or management consulting to gain organizational leadership experience
- "My weaknesses are my GPA and GMAT, non "blue-chip" company. My strengths: essays, work & leadership experiences"
- Born overseas but U.S. raised, unique background with overcoming adversity
- 24-year-old Asian-American immigrant female

Odds of Success:

Stanford (joint degree in School of Education):
15% to 20%
Harvard Business School: 20% to 30%
Berkeley: 40+%
Yale: 50+%
Wharton: 25% to 40%
Northwestern: 40% to 60%
Columbia: 40% to 50%
Duke: 50% to 60%

Sandy's Analysis: Well, you seem to know your own strengths and weaknesses very well, which is the beginning of wisdom, but not, I fear the beginning of being accepted by Stanford or Harvard.

For the reasons you mention–low GPA and lowish GMAT, plus non-blue chip firm—you're asking them to blink twice or maybe 1.5 times, and they will take someone similar to you with better stats and schooling. The rest is real solid, and you have a terrific halo effect from consistent work, in an important field (ed tech is a hot item, even though its benefits have been oversold, but who cares, not your fault) and lots of extras plus a good "Coming to America" story.

I like you, and my guess is, with real solid execution, which should be easy, given how smoothly your goals flow from your experience, you could be real strong candidate at Kellogg, Haas, Yale, and Duke. Wharton may balk because of stats and because you are not their 'type' superficially, although that can sometimes be a wild card advantage. Ditto Columbia, but their gag reflex is a little lower in your case (you might get in) because 1. It is just easier in general, 2. They have a big Ed school, where you'd be a natural fit.

Man, I just read this over, and I like you even more. I'm trying to do some regression analysis (well, what I think that means). And if you had a 3.9 and the company you work for is substantial or serious, you'd be real strong at H or S. The rest of this is just so solid. A neighbor of mine started an educational consulting company right out of Harvard Ed School, doing what seems like what your company does, and he had an HBS grad working for him. Explain the grades in some way and stress international do-gooder stories, and write back and tell me you made it to Harvard or Stanford. Somehow I think your chances are better at Harvard because you have more room to explain yourself, e.g. basically seven story ops plus a goal statement. You could really fill that out.

Ms. Half Minority

- 760 GMAT
- 2.5 – 2.7 GPA
- Undergraduate degree from non-Harvard/Yale/Princeton Ivy
- Have valid medical reason for low GPA
- Worked for four years at a small-by-design market consultancy
- Half minority and dual citizen of a country that will likely have no other applicants to top MBA programs
- Extracurriculars include advising a college women's group and alumni involvement
- "Is the GPA a non-starter for every school?"

Odds of Success:

Harvard Business School: 20%
Stanford: 15%
Wharton: 30+%
Columbia: 30+%
Berkeley: 20+%
Duke: 40% to 50%

Sandy's Analysis: For a moment I read 2.5-2.7 GPA non-HYP Ivy (with valid medical reason) as meaning you had a valid medical reason for not going to H-Y-P. Hmmmmm, allergic to clam chowder, bulldogs and the colors orange and black gives you vertigo (me too!).

But I get it now. That valid medical reason, which somehow got cured by the time you got the 4.0 in post-college coursework, better be a doozy, and if not, you might just say you were immature or probably some combo of the two, e.g. had some substantial medical issues, also did not get help, also was uncertain about academic motivation (made worse by condition), blah,

blah. I don't mean to be flip about any serious medical condition, but I caution you that schools have high defenses about this, since, alas, we live in age when many parents can get doctors to say anything and stories abound about holding kids back from kindergarten for one year so they can be the biggest and smartest in their class. It's step one on a 12,000-step program to get Adrian or Kitten into, ahem, H-Y-P.

The 4.0 is some mitigation but that depends on what courses, how many, and just for the record, I hope none of that 4.0 was "online learning baloney," because adcoms prefer applicants who attend learning events in 3-D, week after week, at some appointed time, and then swallow hard and extrude the material back on a 'curated' (proctored) exam. How come? Duh, 'cause that is exactly what you will be doing when you arrive at business school. You are not applying for the paintball team.

The 760 GMAT might be the wind beneath your Hail Mary pass. For our International and secular readers, a Hail Mary pass is http://en.wikipedia. org/wiki/Hail_Mary_pass.

Hard to get a read on your job: "Four years at a small-by-design market leader niche industry consultancy (run by an alum of one of the top-5 MBA programs)" but I salute your jam-packed writing style. Seriously. As noted prior, questions to ask in this case is what track record does that firm have in placing folks into schools. Sounds like a serious place but if schools have no track record there, you need to make clear its virtues and exclusivity.

Half-minority? My dear, when it comes to minority status, as with medical conditions, we round up. Especially if you have real ties to a minority community in terms of activities, etc. Dual citizen of bizarro country, "that will likely have no other applicants to top MBA programs?" Hmmm, that could be an attraction all by itself, especially if you have your own Internet domain (hbsguru.:-$) But more importantly it could support your half-minority upgrade if you are half-White and Half-Kirabiti. OK, ABOUT YOUR GPA BEING, AS YOU SAY, "A NON-STARTER."

Hard to say, it is not a non-starter, but it is a real, real issue because you are otherwise silver and not gold in terms of employment pedigree, extracurriculars, and anything else they care about. I will revise that if the half-minority issue is actually powerful, if your firm has connections or visibility with schools, if you have some documented heart-breaking medical condition, which is now no longer an impediment to doing good work, as 4.0 indicates, and if your admirably terse prose is also reflective of your focus.

But this is an interesting exercise. Let's say you had 3.6, you'd still be a longish shot at HBS and Stanford because there is nothing driving you in, no stardust, no powerful one extra or set of extras. Lots of people from H-Y-P with 760 and 3.6 with the rest of your stats do not get into HBS or Stanford so why are they going to take you, even if they accommodate the medical issue? Columbia is pretty number focused, although one number they may focus on is the 760.

So, I'm calling that a reach. Wharton is not known for taking off-the-grid cases, despite what they claim, so I'm calling that a reach plus. Duke and Haas, that might be possible. Once they blink at the GPA, everything else is up their alley. I'm being speculative here, so feel free to write back after you get into all those places, and call me whatever you want.

A lot will turn on how compelling your medical story is, and to some degree, how juiced-up any adcom in a daring mindset will be, especially if she dreams of using you as teaser bait at Future Forums where she proudly proclaims to the goober wannabes, "We took a kid last year with a 2.5 GPA! See anyone can get in." And believe me, the adcom will say that, and not mention the medical condition or the 760 or 4.0, and she will be fibbing through her teeth, but nonetheless, you will be in.

Mr. KPMG

- 660 GMAT
- 3.86 GPA
- Undergraduate degree in business from Ithaca College
- Consultant with KPMH Advisory for two years, former financial analyst at The Walt Disney Co.
- Extracurricular activity includes being president of the student-run mutual fund while at Ithaca

---

Odds of Success:

Harvard Business School: Less than 20%
Wharton: 20%
Chicago: Less than 50%
Dartmouth: Less than 50%
Cornell: 50%
Yale: 50%

Sandy's Analysis: Dude, assuming you took the GMAT less than five times in the past year, keep taking it until you hit five or 700. Also try the GRE. Ithaca College is an out-of-the-way place that schools like to brag they don't overlook (calling Dee Leopold!!!), but a high GPA and low-ish GMAT makes it seem like the GPA is the fluke. KPMG is an okay but second-tier job in this racket, but Walt Disney is gold, even if being a financial analyst is less classy than being in business development (the home of the Ivy/IB/pre-HBS crowd).

The GMAT will keep you out of Wharton, while with a 710, you could be in the running there based on the Disney glow. I'm not seeing this as an HBS admit, although again a 700+ GMAT and some powerful execution

146

on extras we could beat out of you might make it a 20 percent chance. Booth, Tuck, Cornell and Yale might go for you in present form based on Disney, GPA and maybe some explanation of the GMAT score.

General note to low GMAT scorers: You need to explain the score and you need to take the test at least twice to show that you tried. For example, if this dude took the GMAT three times and he ain't going to do any better, he needs to explain why he can do the math in a top B-school program. A 660 always requires taking the test twice just to show you care.

Mr. Cancer Survivor

- 740 GMAT
- 3.9 GPA
- Undergraduate degree in accounting from a competitive private school
- Survived cancer during freshman year of college and have been actively involved in pediatric cancer advocacy ever since
- Work experience includes one and one-half years at a major consulting firm (LEK/Monitor) and two years at a well-known, mid-market private equity shop in Boston
- Extracurricular involvement in significant leadership positions during a two-year service mission for his church in Northern California; also founded and directed a tutoring program to help inmates earn GED diplomas; Eagle Scout, president of alumni chapter and volunteer in pediatric cancer unit of children's hospital
- Goals: To get back into private equity PE and help grow medium-sized businesses
- "Not to be cynical, but how do I leverage my cancer story to my advantage? Have you seen this done successfully before? What makes the white male consultant/PE guy stand out in a crowded field of so many with a similar profile?"
- 27-year-old, married white male

Odds of Success:

Harvard: 30% to 45%
Stanford: 15% to 20%
Wharton: 40% to 50%
Chicago: 50+%
MIT: 40% to 50%

Sandy's Analysis: Guys like you get into Harvard Business School without cancer stories. You got a solid record and scores and LEK/Monitor class employment is good starter situation. I assume your current PE shop is also good feeder firm. You are an interesting contrast to the guy above you, and you are how peeps with accounting degrees get into HBS. Somehow you wound up at LEK/Monitor, and he wound up in the Big 4. That could be the critical difference.

As to your questions, surviving cancer is not as big a plus as you might think (what else were you supposed to do?) What really matters is what you did afterwards by becoming a cancer advocate. That does register as an excellent extra, since it impacts people beyond yourself and you seem to have taken a leadership role. HBS also likes helping prison inmates–your other strong extra–some of whom might have been HBS grads unbeknownst to you. There are certainly enough HBS cons and ex-cons around, not to mention a very large group of HBS grads who would be in jail if that were determined by general election and not judges. But I am getting light headed.

You got a real strong story in toto. As to your questions, how to spin the cancer issue? You can use your cancer story as a setback you overcame. HBS sees lots of essays like that, some better than others, depending on the core facts and on what you draw out of the experience. And you can use your volunteer work with cancer patients as an accomplishment, or you can combine both into the last 400-word essay, sort of I WISH YOU ASKED ME ABOUT MY CANCER AND WHAT FOLLOWED. So you can play it lots of different ways.

Sometimes "big" personal stories like cancer, losing buddies in war (by military guys), suicide of friends or parents, and AIDS, really register hard and sometimes those stories don't, and are treated respectfully but not really as a super value add. It is a real interesting phenomenon, and it depends on your execution of the story itself and your take away, as well as how it synchs up with everything else in your app. I think you will score a hit with your work with pediatric cancer patients because it links up with the entire service theme in your story.

You're a guy with real good GPA/GMAT stats who has lots of extras, especially for a guy in consulting/PE, where current extras are often thin. HBS takes guys like you all the time, and also dings them if 1. You get unlucky, 2. Someone thinks you are trying too hard, despite all the do-gooder stuff. Asking the very questions you asked could be a hint of that possibly happening, although I appreciate your honesty and the occasion to opine on how to game this – adcoms smelling that same wind may declare foul. That is what you got to watch out for.

As noted many times (something I seem to be saying many times) getting into HBS is more about FITTING IN rather than STANDING OUT. You got great grades and GMAT, you work for solid firms, you got solid extras—that is fitting in. You don't need cancer, although sure, you had it, so live it up.

Just don't let it kill your app. That would be one way cancer would get the last laugh.

Mr. Healthcare

- 700 GMAT (will be retaking)
- 3.25 GPA (have taken two courses since and gotten As)
- Undergraduate degree in biology and economics from Brown University
- Work experience includes five years in health care strategy consulting, three at a boutique firm and two at a major management consulting firm. Have a track record of excellent performance reviews, team leadership and client satisfaction
- Heavily involved in extracurricular activity at school, including multiple mentoring positions, leadership jobs and volunteer programs

---

Odds of Success:

Wharton: 20% to 30%
Northwestern: 25% to 40%
NYU: 30%
Chicago: 25% to 40%
Duke: 35% to 50%
Columbia: 40% (early decision)

Sandy's Analysis: Well, except for your low-ish GPA and 700 GMAT, you are a solid guy with an Ivy education and what appears to be two solid jobs. I assume the boutique job is the current one? Taking those two extra courses is helpful, and if you are dead set on Wharton, you might take two more. Also, while I don't usually advise retaking a 700 GMAT, in your case, I do, if you have your heart set on Philly. They get a lot of guys just like you (Ivy, solid jobs, solid extras) and the raw numbers often make deciding real easy, even if they should not.

Solid execution as to why you want an MBA and why now will also help (five years of consulting experience is on the high side), along with some focused but dream-filtered goal statement. Even with your present stats, guys like you get in and dinged from Kellogg and Booth, and mostly get in to Duke (if you convince them they are not sloppy fifths). Not sure I see the NYU fit. Jack up the GMAT and try Columbia early decision.

Ms. Consultant

- 700 GMAT
- 3.6 GPA
- Undergraduate degree in political science from Ivy U.
- Work experience includes three years at a top consulting firm
- Extracurricular involvement as volunteer of a mentorship program for abused women, concert pianist, vice president of class, and manager of college house
- Goal: To work in corporate strategy for consumer products/retail with a focus on Asian markets
- Plan to apply for an MA/MBA dual program in 2012
- 24-year-old Asian female and U.S. permanent resident

Odds of Success:

Harvard: 30+%
Wharton: 50+%
MIT: 40% to 50+%
Columbia: 50+%
NYU: 60+%

Sandy's Analysis: This also is a classic profile, viz. Ivy 3.6, 700 GMAT, and 'top' consulting experience– and beyond that what appear to be lots of extras. And a classical pianist!!! You are sort of a solid consulting kid, which is very solid indeed, with a couple of pluses and minuses: more extracurrics than many top consultants, and probably a lower GMAT but one (700) good enough for most schools. A lot will depend on the level of support you get from your firm in terms of recommendations. That is a key issue. Big 3 consulting firm (McKinsey, BCG, and Bain) kids get dinged from H/S/W when they get tepid support from the firm or blow the interview (that is sometimes legit—several consulting kids are weird), and sometimes just bad luck. Other reasons Big 3 consulting firm kids get dinged is just lackluster careers, or poor presentation of careers, and subpar extras compared to their very talented peers.

Your goals are fine. So it is just a matter of execution and firm support and luck. If you will have four years of consulting firm experience at matriculation, that is at the border. Five is really excessive and B-schools begin to believe you are being pushed out. I am not sure what you mean by "MA/MBA" dual degree, what subject are you seeking an MA in??? Phew, I would rethink that one, given your story and goals.

"Goal: To work in corporate strategy for consumer products/retail with a focus on Asian markets."

Jeepers, just a little ol' MBA will serve you fine for that goal, and save you thousands of dollars and a good deal of demented class time rubbing shoulders with some terminal MA types.

Mr. Airline

- 710 GMAT
- 3.76 GPA
- Undergraduate degree in finance from Brigham Young University
- Work experience includes one year at a boutique litigation consulting firm, valuing lost profits and developing/rebutting expert testimony, and two at an airline company developing a labor analysis group and negotiating with union groups. Also had undergraduate internships with Citigroup in Tokyo and Johnson & Johnson and spent two years as a Mormon missionary in Tokyo
- Extracurricular activities include head coaching a middle school lacrosse team, various church activities, and Boy Scouts.
- Goal: To join an aircraft leasing firm in an operations or finance role or to join an aviation consulting/advisory firm

---

Odds of Success:

Harvard: 10% to 25%
MIT: 25+%
Wharton: 30% to 45+%
Dartmouth: 30% to 45+%
Duke: 50+%
Virginia: 50+%

Sandy's Analysis: This is a "just-off" HBS/LDS profile because your jobs are off the beaten path and goals are too narrow. Also, hold onto your hat, a 3.76 could be in the lower half of BYU GPA HBS admits. Lots of HBS admits seem to roll out of BYU with 3.9's etc. but that is a subtle point. The real thing that is going to make HBS hard is your off-the-grid and, possibly to them, not super-selective jobs. Your type of litigation and labor consulting IS represented at HBS but usually those candidates work for blue chip firms in those fields, not boutiques.

Even if you get past those subtle and never-spoken prejudices, there is nothing driving you into the school in terms of stardust. For purely gaming-the-system purposes, you should have continued on at either Citigroup in Tokyo (a real plus) or J&J, a classic HBS feeder firm. Wharton, MIT, Tuck, Duke and Virginia are all in range given your solid stats and your pretty solid story plus the Japan angle, which is impressive in general. Unfortunately it does not synch up with your goals. That's another reason you would have been better at Citi with a story about doing banking in Asia, if getting into HBS is all that matters to you. Then, POOF, it all fits together.

At all schools, I might say you are interested in strategy consulting, not aviation consulting, per se. Or just phrase your goals more broadly. Being that specific is something you do when you are applying above your head, and you want to assure the school that you will be employable. You don't need that card and some schools might object to you using them to get your "ticket punched" at your old job rather than being open to an, ahem, "transformational experience." The only exception to that might be MIT, which has expertise in aviation and even a wind tunnel.

Ms. Education

- 720 GMAT
- 3.5 GPA
- Undergraduate degree from the University of Virginia
- Work Experience includes two years in higher education consulting, focusing on business and finance issues facing top-tier universities, and one year as an analyst at a boutique consulting firm specializing in philanthropic investment strategy.
- Extracurricular involvement as the three-year president of an annual fundraising event at university; chaired the giving campaign for my graduating class; led a 200-volunteer program that matched students with high-need local schools). In past two years, I've mentored an at-risk middle schooler, performed social work case management with the homeless, and am involved with a pro bono consulting group
- Goals: "To bring the rigor of business and management principles to higher education management, particularly in the community college space."
- 24-year-old woman

Odds of Success:

Harvard: 35+%
Stanford: 20%
Wharton: 35+%
Dartmouth: 45+%
Northwestern: 50%

Sandy's Analysis: Lots of pep here, in a good way. Your 3.5 at UVA and 720 GMAT are good enough for most places. A lot of your outcomes may turn on work experience, which is hard to sniff out from your descriptions. You say, "2 years in higher education consulting, focusing on business and finance issues facing top-tier universities; 1 year as an analyst at a boutique consulting firm specializing in philanthropic investment strategy." HMMMM, that could mean a good deal in terms of selectivity, visibility to schools, etc. And, ahem, which of those jobs is CURRENT?

It would be better in terms of your story if the current job is the higher ed consulting one, although I am not sure what exactly, "focusing on business and finance issues facing top-tier universities" means. I am familiar with consulting firms, which focus on managing/advising on university endowments and those are well thought of by B- schools. As usual, an easy way for you to answer this question is to look around at where people who had your job wound up going to B-school over the past three years.

Your intense extra-currics will be a plus at most places, especially HBS, Stanford and Kellogg, and so will a career that seems focused on education, universities and community service. I'm less sure about saying you want to focus on community colleges, although that does comport with my usual goal advice– find a space within your space as a nominal focus point. My fear is that most MBA admissions boards may find community colleges infra dig. I'd say you are real interested in finding ways to re-engineer the educational experience to make it accessible and pragmatic, and that could mean working with new models of two-year experiences or four-year or some new paradigm still being born.

The "status" of your current employer is the big unknown in making predictions, but if you are working for a legitimate and recognized player in higher-ed consulting, you got a chance at most top schools, with HBS and Stanford requiring boffo execution, so all your strengths come together.

Mr. Consultant in Germany

- 730 GMAT
- 3.7 GPA
- Undergraduate degree in economics and business from a German University with a semester abroad at an Ivy League school
- Work experience includes work for a global top five consulting company in Germany after interning at a small hedge fund, bulge bracket investment bank in equity sales, and at another consulting company
- Extracurricular involvement as a volunteer in a children's ministry at church and a year doing community service in the U.S.
- Goal: To "move to the U.S. and either work in consulting or for a start up. Hope to launch my own start-up later or work in a non-profit

Odds of Success:

Harvard: 20-35%
Wharton: 30% to 45%
Stanford: 15-20%
Columbia: 30% to 50%
Kellogg: 30% to 50%
Chicago: 30% to 40+%
Berkeley: 50%
MIT: 30%

Sandy's Analysis: Hmmm, real solid across the board. A lot will depend on how your consulting company is viewed by those schools, and the best way to figure that out is to find out what its record is in MBA admissions over the past one to four years. This may seem like common sense but it is an inquiry frequently overlooked. HR may keep track of this, or you may need to make some polite inquiries to fellow workers in the U.S.

Another issue may be what you do, e.g. strategic consulting versus account-ing, with a preference at U.S. business schools for strategic consulting. So whatever you do, make it sound like strategy consulting, and if, in fact, that IS what you do, well, make sure that comes across. Germans used to be "rare-ish" at HBS, e.g. there were only seven German passport holders in the class of 2001, while that number typically runs to 14 per class over the past three years.

(As a comparison, France had 19 in the Class in 2001 and 12 more recently; someone explain this to me? Is Dee a closet Germanophile? I don't think so. It might have something to do with the perceived value of a Harvard MBA in Germany, and who knows, the reunion of East and West Germany).

I am not sure that saying you plan to "move to the U.S." as part of your goal statement would add anything. You should try to generate substantive goals, e.g. alternative energy consulting (just to pick a current cliché), and then let the geography chips fall where they may. Nor is your end point, "later, work in non-profit" – that just sounds pasted on, and in combina-tion with work in U.S., it sounds like you are just generically smart and ambitious.

I got no beef with that but schools prefer applicants who feign wanting to impact the world and not just their own place in the world. A small issue, you seem like a totally nice guy, but you will be competing against some equally accomplished but app-savvy guys and gals, and at real selective places (H/S/W) that could make a difference.

Once you mildly sculpt your story, as suggested, your chances at Harvard and Stanford are in the GLY . . . range (Guys Like You Get Dinged and Guys Like You Get Admitted –depending on execution, recommenda-tions, luck, and not blowing the interview). Wharton takes kids like you with solid execution. Columbia would be a solid place, as would others you mention.

Mr. Hedge Fund

- 720 GMAT
- 3.7 GPA
- Undergraduate degree in economics from a little Ivy college (Williams/Amherst/Swat)
- Work experience includes two years at Bain Consulting before transitioning into an equity hedge fund for about 3.5 years
- Extracurricular includes being president and founder of a number of clubs, sat on a number of advisory boards to college executive leadership (diversity boards, career services boards, lecture committees). Also had a hand in developing alumni relationships for the career services.
- Goal: "Starting a full service investment management boutique."
- "Mostly wondering if I'm already too experienced to make a run at the MBA."
- 26-year-old Chinese born in the U.S.

Odds of Success:

Harvard: 20-30%
Stanford: 10-20%
Wharton: 40-50+%
Columbia: 40-50+%
MIT: 30+%

Sandy's Analysis: Do I have this right: five/six years of experience, two at Bain, and then since 2008 at an equity hedge fund? That could be a real issue at HBS and also Stanford, where they begin to distrust applicants that far out based on some mildly nutty theory (a rare screwy bee in Harvard Dean Nohira's bonnet) that applicants over X years in banking/finance are somehow being shipped off to business school as a sop for not being promoted to Junior Master of the Universe.

Now just what equals "X years experience" in this formula is an issue, and less of an issue with you since you have only been in finance for four years, and X is less than that. But the two years at Bain might get unfairly stapled onto that, in some wacky thought system (which adcoms are subject to) so that is the way your work history could bite you.

All the rest is solid, although let me add, for general readers, not sure if this applies to you per se, that extras having to do with alum clubs, and the board work you seem to have a long list of, are good but not as good as outright engagements and ladling soup at do-gooder orgs with an impact far removed from yourself. Beware of seeming too much like a board networker and not a genuine do-gooder.

Columbia should fall into place. Sloan will like how solid all this is, and they are the last place standing which welcomes applicants interested in financial engineering, which it seems like what you do. Sorry if I misread that, but they will like what you do anyway. The issue at Harvard and Stanford is the too-much experience and lack of impactful do-gooder extras, although difficult to say how big an issue that will be.

Mr. Peace Corps

- 720 GMAT
- 3.63 Grade Point Average
- Undergraduate degree in finance from Miami University
- Work experience includes a year as a process consultant for a mid-sized regional firm in Chicago and two-plus years in the Peace Corps in Uganda where I founded a local fair trade social enterprise which was nominated as a Peace Corps Uganda success story of the year, founded micro-finance associations, co-founded vocational training center, micro-consulting
- Extracurricular involvement as chief editor of the Peace Corps newsletter in Uganda; a tutor for an African-heritage focused public school in the U.S. and for Sudanese Lost Boys
- Goal: Short-term is to be a strategic consultant; long-term is to establish a firm that provides seed investing and strategic/financial consulting for Sub-Sahara African startups
- 26-year-old white male

Odds of Success:

Stanford: 20% to 30%
Berkeley: 40% to 50%
Northwestern: 30% to 50%
UCLA: 50+%
Chicago: 30% to 40%

Sandy's Analysis: Hmmmm, let's call this a real solid Peace Corp career in Uganda with a 3.6 from a good school and a 720 GMAT. Stanford may not find that recherche enough, especially for a white male. I'd be interested if someone could spill out the Peace Corp cohort at Stanford, but my guess is, it's part Ivy, it's part minority, and it's got lotsa anchor jobs (like

McKinsey) in the mix (versus your "unanchor" gig at "mid-sized regional firm in Chicago," which sounds like The Office was filmed there).

All that snark aside, you got a 15% to 20% chance there given what appear to be great works you performed in Uganda (are you still in Peace Corp now?), if you can spin that in some Stanford-y way. Chances at Haas, Kellogg and Anderson are solid, based on stats (3.6/720) alone. Throw Booth in the mix too, they love social enterprise jive. Well, who doesn't?

Mr. Consultant

- 660 GMAT (Taken it twice and not sure I have time to take again)
- 3.4 GPA
- Undergraduate degree from Brigham Young University in business management
- Work Experience includes two years at a process-consulting firm, worked on some healthcare clients (think Big Four consulting, not strategy) one year as an internal auditor for a national health plan (Kaiser Permanente, Blue Cross, United Health Care)
- Extracurricular involvement includes a two-year church mission to Australia, was vice president of the business school student association, organized an annual charity auction and volunteered for Habitat for Humanity
- Goal: "I'm passionate about the healthcare industry and its (many) unique challenges. I plan to use an MBA to facilitate a move away from audit and towards healthcare consulting (provider side). Specifically, im interested in helping organizations manage and plan for the effects of healthcare reform."
- "Do you think I have a shot at any of the above in light of my low GMAT score? Or better to wait until next year?"
- 26-year-old white male

Odds of Success:

Duke (dream school): 30%
UCLA: 20% to 30%
Northwestern: 25%
Vanderbilt: 50%

Sandy's Analysis: Aside from a low GMAT and a low GPA, you're a totally likeable guy. And actually, average GPA at Duke, your dream school, is 3.4.

Alas, their median GMAT is 696 so the question becomes do you have 36 GMAT points (a lot!!) worth of charm. Let me give you some tough love. B-schools are mildly biased in favor of Mormons because the LDS values of family, hard work, sobriety and honesty are in synch with generic business values. Also, my guess is, most schools' experiences with LDS members are positive. So that is a small plus.

After that, doing a mission is kind of baked in (even if not all LDS kids do so) and Australia is not ranked as high on the value chain as a country where you operate in a more foreign language and culture. Your extras, even though Church related, seem real solid, even by LDS standards, so that is a plus. The fact you are working in a health care environment is positive, but offset by the fact that it seems to be, in your own words, "process" and "auditing" centric.

Shake all that up in our Duke-tini mixer and what do we got??? Close one, but I am calling it more likely "no" than "yes." One decider is the fact of your low Quant score on the GMAT. If you tweaked this, with a 680 GMAT and a mission to Latin America, and being president of the Business School Association instead of vice-president, you'd have a fighting chance of having them blink at the GMAT and Second Tier work gigs at solid companies. In your present incarnation, there is nothing driving you in, and the cherry on the non-alcoholic Duke-tini ding is being white male. Anderson is actually tougher than Duke to get into, so I'm not optimistic there either. Ditto Kellogg. Vanderbilt is totally in-line stat wise, so you got a real solid chance there.

I don't see any downside in applying to the whole menu this year, especially Duke, sometimes those schools get to know you through the application process, and that can help next year. I would also find a great GMAT tutor, focus only on the Quant part, and see if you can get another 5 questions right. Some more ideas are to think about taking the GRE's instead. You might find the Quant on that exam a bit easier or different. If you are really gung-ho, and cannot move the needle with the standardized testing, take some real solid math courses over the summer to develop an alternative transcript.

The Bankers

Applicants from investment banks, investment management firms, private equity and venture capital shops typically account for the largest single group of students at most of the elite business schools. Just look at Wharton's entering class in 2011: MBA candidates with financial backgrounds made up 42% of the incoming students. Roughly 16% of the class were from private equity and venture capital firms, while 14% came from investment banks alone.

At the University of Chicago's Booth School of Business and Columbia Business School, just about one in every three incoming students had a financial background. At Harvard, it was one in four. At Stanford, some 29% of the incoming students in 2011 came from financial services, with 17% of the class having worked for either a venture capital fund or a private equity shop.

The following profiles give you a sense of how varied these financial candidates are and also how Sandy suggests they position themselves to shift the odds in their favor. A good number of financial types also fall into the poet and quant categories as well.

Ms. Ivy Cheerleader

- 770 GMAT
- 3.9 GPA
- Undergraduate degree in economics and math from an Ivy League school
- Work experience includes three years as a trader at a top bulge bracket investment banking firm, with stints in both the U.S. and Eastern Europe
- Extracurricular involvement included cheerleading (president and treasurer), gymnastics, sorority, and lots of community work, with a strong connection to cancer (meaningful personal drama as a kid)

> **Odds of Success:**
>
> Harvard Business School: 50%+
> Stanford: 40% to 50%
> Wharton: 70%+

Sandy's Analysis: Hmmmmm, got a photo? I'm sure plenty of even healthy P&Q readers might be curious about cheerleaders with 770 GMATs and an Ivy 3.9. This sounds like a slam dunk at Wharton, just based on stats and interests, although see caveat about goals.

Applicants like you get dinged at HBS if you mishandle the leadership aspects and make them sound banal, or blow the interview, or fail to execute on goals or give a weak reason why you want or need an MBA. The weakness in the above, to the extent that there is any, is that trading is disfavored activity at Harvard and Stanford, because it does not logically lead to an MBA or provide a platform for any meaningful activity, in their humble opinions. So you will need to be careful with that.

I would not say that you want to grow up into a bigger trader, and e.g., buying Acme at 30 and selling it at 150 does not score very high as an accomplishment at HBS, although maybe saying how you talked stupid males on the trading floor to get behind this deal, does. Dealing with stupid men at work always a winner for smart women, especially the super Type-A variety one imagines (from movies) are traders.

At Stanford, where they are not nuts about traders either, you could blow it by just not putting together a meaningful "What Matters Most" essay. I would not say buying low and selling high. You seem to have a lot of personal stories and extras to work on, and allude, in the above, to a meaningful personal drama with cancer as a kid, so that could be a place to start, but sometimes what seems like easy topics are the hardest to execute.

Try isolating what you learned from cancer survivors or their families or how the experience impacted your family. "Learning" moments are what Stanford likes.

Mr. Finance (not in New York)

- 700 GMAT
- 3.5 GPA
- Undergraduate degree from a top 30 state school with a double major in finance and economics
- Work experience includes a year at the Federal Reserve Bank doing financial analysis and two and one-half years (at matriculation) working in portfolio risk management at a GSE.
- I'm ranked in the top 1% of performers in the company
- Extracurricular activity includes being the founder of a national leadership development fraternity, the division lead for Help the Homeless fundraising, and multiple honors societies with little or no participation ("Are they even worth mentioning in my applications?")
- Career goals: To work in asset liability management role, making investment decisions (trader) and to eventually become a Treasurer at a non-New York finance firm.
- 26-years-old (at matriculation)

Odds of Success:

Wharton (I know it's a long shot): Yes, it is!
Virginia: 30%
Duke: 30%
North Carolina: 30+%
Georgetown: 40% to 50%

Sandy's Analysis: Being ranked in the top 1 percent in a Federal Reserve cohort is impressive to me. I like the top one percent of almost everything, and so may most of the schools you apply to. But this is not like being ranked in the top one percent of say, not GSE, but just plain ol' GS.

You said, "Career goals: Work in asset liability management role making investment decisions (trader) and eventually become a Treasurer at a non-New York finance firm." Apparently they are not going to have any trouble keeping you down on the farm after you have seen New York, or have you?

Non-New York finance firm? Well, they do exist, and if you are just being honest with us readers here, and would not say something that odd to a school, well, okay. But do note that being allergic to New York City is not a plus on any application, even one to Keenan-Flagler. It is certainly a negative at Wharton, where they consider New York City their week-end apartment.

All right, down to basics: a 700 and a 3.5 is "close enough for government work" at Fuqua, Darden, K-F, and Georgetown, and government work is certainly what you got. So, I'm predicting success at those places unless you go oddball on them, a possibility given self-presentation wrinkles in the above, just a vibe I'm getting from the way you describe goals and some other things.

If, in fact, you are the toast of Toastmasters and the designated emcee at most weddings, I apologize. Certainly your impressive extras, both the active and inactive ones, will help. "Multiple honors societies but with little/no participation (are they even worth mentioning in application?)"

Answer: It depends. If it appears you are an honor society fetishist, no. Otherwise, maybe.

More seriously, I would clarify goals to be of a more executive material. After the smoke clears, it appears you want to be a trader. Well, trader is one of those things that many MBA's wind up doing after graduation but few applicants actually say they want to do going in. An MBA will not make you a better trader. Wharton? Phew, you have a lowish GMAT for them and an average GPA at a Tier 2-3 school, along with a huckleberry hound job even with a one percent rating. I agree with you, long shot.

Mr. IB

- 740 GMAT
- 3.9 GPA
- Undergraduate degree with double major in accounting and finance from a top 40 public university (think Southern football school)
- Work experience at a "brand name bulge bracket investment bank" as a controller
- Extracurricular involvement holding a leadership position for a selective club that worked directly with the dean and a leadership position for a professional business fraternity
- Goal: "I want to break into IB and eventually VC to pursue funding educational tech companies focusing or revamping and redesigning America's educational system. Our education infrastructure is out of touch with the changing demands of the twenty first century and we need private companies to lead the way because government is dropping the ball."
- 26-year-old white male

Odds of Success:

Harvard Business School: 20% to 30%
Stanford: 15%
Wharton: 30% to 50%
Chicago: 35% to 55%
MIT: 35%
Berkeley: 30% to 60%
Duke: 40% to 60+%
Virginia: 40% to 60+%

Sandy's Analysis: Real simple question, and maybe you can help us: "How many kids from your function/office at the investment bank have ever applied to B-school and what are the outcomes?" That is your best metric. If the answer is 20 over the past three years, well, snooping around those 20 stories and gut checking the outcomes will tell you if you are getting into HBS.

Although, based on your stats, if anyone ever got into HBS, you will too, unless that other person was a minority or had some other exceptional victim-helper story. As noted, also many times, one key consideration for top schools is how hard is your job to get? Is it harder than landing a job at the Big Four? My thinking is yes. All that said, the reason you won't get into HBS or Stanford is that you are too boring—from their point of view.

I find working with the dean, leadership in business frats, and professional mentoring riveting, but schools like Stanford and HBS somehow prefer it if you do things which impact communities more alien to your home turf. There is nothing driving you into those schools, and you actually might have a hard time getting into Harvard or Stanford with this profile even if you were in real IB (certainly into Stanford).

At Wharton, with solid execution, it could happen because numbers are real solid. For sure, you are in line at Booth, Haas, Fuqua, and Darden, although you may have to really put your best suit and tie on at Booth, for reasons similar to HBS. This ain't smelling like a Sloan admit, but they have been known to fall for white bread guys covered with very high stats as jam, which could be you.

As to your stated goals: "I want to break into IB and eventually VC to pursue funding educational tech companies focusing or revamping and redesigning America's educational system. Our education infrastructure is out of touch with the changing demands of the twenty first century and we need private companies to lead the way because government is dropping the ball." Hmmm, you need to find out the PC way to say the same thing. Channeling Ron Paul is not good for applicants.

Mr. Finance

- 710 GMAT
- 3.7 GPA
- Undergraduate degree from Richard Ivey School of Business in Canada.
- Work experience includes three years at J.P. Morgan on the fixed income desk managing corporate pension plans; currently senior product management associate at PIMCO
- Extracurricular involvement includes alumni mentoring programs and intramural sports.
- 27-year-old Taiwanese-Canadian male

Odds of Success:

Harvard Business School: 25% to 35%
Chicago: 30% to 50%
Wharton: 40+%
Columbia: 50% to 60%

Sandy's Analysis: Columbia early admission should be very doable given solid stats, blue chip work history and focus on one of their strengths (finance). PIMCO is a real solid place to apply from ever since Bill Gross, the CEO, started appearing on TV and Mo El-Erian, the number two guy at PIMCO, ditched leading the Harvard endowment to go back there (he is also on TV a lot).

HBS takes kids from Pimco but they gotta be more interesting than you (see comments on last guy). Wharton is like 40+ percent, with impactful execution. They would like the Pimco brand and the rest is in line.

If you are applying to Columbia, it is real important to take the tour, and show a commitment to New York, like by living there in the first place. I know, you said early decision, which is one way to show commitment. Dual degree with public policy? What's with that? It just does not compute with the rest of your story.

NYU should happen, Chicago is 50+. You are in their wheelhouse. Ahem, one assumes you will apply to those other schools if you do not get into Columbia ED, and if you do, you will attend.

Mr. Bulge Bracket

- 700 GMAT
- 3.1 GPA
- Undergraduate degree in economics from Fordham University
- Work experience includes three years at a "top performing but unknown" hedge fund
- Extracurricular involvement includes active leadership role in college alumni organization, member of an NYC private club.
- Goal: To gain "a client-facing position at a bulge bank on the wealth management side."
- 26-years-old at matriculation

Odds of Success:

Virginia: 20%
Dartmouth: 20%
Cornell: 30% to 55%
Texas: 40% to 60%
Georgetown: 50+%
New York: 70% (part-time)

Sandy's Analysis: Darden and Tuck are not going to bite because your stats and story are just too low for them, unless someone at your Hedge Fund or your private club in New York City can pull a string. Cornell takes guys like you, although near the bottom the deck, so you got a 30 to 55% chance there. Texas ditto, but they are maybe just a little more GPA conscious, Georgetown is the flip side of that coin, so chances there are better. NYU part time should not be that hard. Wealth Management is good goal to say to these places, and make it clear you won't have a hard time getting that job. Otherwise, if they hear you want to join a bulge bracket firm, they may just put you in the 'seen-the-Wall-Street-movies-too-many-times' basket.

Basically ALL schools, and especially ones you are targeting, don't want unemployed grads. So you need to make it real clear that based on x, y and z of your career so far, getting a Wealth Management gig will not be hard.

Here is another, ahem, tip. You might just tell them Wealth Management and skip the bulge bracket wording. Bulge bracket is often what dreaming schmucks say at 2nd tier places to sound "with it." It's a real turn-off to adcoms, probably because they have, over time, met the actual candidates who say that, and those meetings have just confirmed their initial distaste. The cultured among us, including moi, say "leading investment banks." The fact that real people on Wall St. may or may not say bulge bracket is, as you might guess, of absolutely zero to possibly negative interest to an admissions officer, especially one at a bulge bracket school.

Ahem, having a bulge in your package may help you with the buff babes at the gym, but having a bulge in your admissions package is no way to get a date with Ms. Darden, Tuck, or Johnson.

Mr. Derivatives

- 710 GMAT
- 3.83 Grade Point Average
- Undergraduate degree from Brigham Young University-Idaho (current president is former dean of Harvard Business School
- Work Experience includes a year and one-half at a small derivatives trading firm; two and one-half years starting a derivatives trading and investment management firm.
- Extracurricular activities include two years service as a missionary in Asia, including positions of leadership for up to 15 individuals, co-captain of intra-collegiate basketball team, various church leadership positions(president of congregation's Sunday School, president of men's quorum), participation in other clubs. Continued church participation and leadership post-undergrad, church basketball participation.
- Goal: "I want to get back into trading or investment management (but with a large established firm) utilizing my past experience with derivatives.

Odds of Success:

Harvard Business School: 20% to 30%
Stanford: 15% to 20%
Wharton: 25% to 35%
Chicago: 40+%
Kellogg: 40+%

Sandy's Analysis: Well, if Kim Clark, the former HBS dean and now president of BYU-Idaho wants to spend one of his two or three chips a year on you, you will get into HBS. Of course, I don't know how many chips he actually has or spends, but you get the idea, if he wants to make it happen, it will happen.

Let's assume that is not going to be the case: HBS is not going to like this work profile. They have a bias against traders and "derivatives" is a dirty word over there. Working as a broker at some regular outfit, which sells derivatives (as your note stated) is not a typical HBS flight path either. The grades and GMAT are fine, the extras are in line with LDS kids they see, maybe LDS plus one, but that is not going to tip this at HBS. There, they will take Mormons with better work gigs, and my guess, from BYU-Utah. Does anyone know the record of BYU-Idaho kids into H/S/W? Same analysis at Stanford. I don't see you getting in there, either. Jobs are second-tier and nothing super driving you in. Wharton takes kids like you, but lots apply, so it is a matter of breaking out of the congestion. You need to execute there in a way that is impressive but doesn't get too preachy.

Assume Wharton application reader will be a secular humanist. Chances at Booth and Kellogg are in-line, same advice as Wharton, and quite frankly, I'd go light on the derivatives at all those places. Financial engineering or making money out of nothing is not a winning topic with B-school adcoms these days, despite what faculty and alums might think. You need a new story. You'll want to use financial experience and transition into advisory role as a consultant or maybe an investment banker. If you say IB, be sure to point out, at schools like Chicago and Kellogg, and also Columbia, that you have spoken to insiders in that field and you have a career path. That way, it is not just daydreaming.

Mr. Gay PE

- 720 GMAT
- 3.8 GPA
- Undergraduate degree from Stanford University in economics
- Worked for two years in investment banking with Goldman Sachs in New York, followed by two years at a top private equity firm in New York
- Extracurricular involvement includes being co-president of a large ethnic student organization at Stanford, leadership role in GS Asian Professionals Network
- Gay Asian-American male
- 25 years old

Odds of Success:

Harvard: 60+%
Stanford: 60+%
Wharton: 70+%
MIT: 70+%
Chicago: 80%
Columbia: 80%

Sandy's Analysis: Don't know what to say, man, do you think being gay will keep you out of Harvard, Stanford or Wharton? It won't. The question I always ask guys like you: "How did other applicants to H/S/W fare at your "top PE firm in NY" last year, and what is the explanation of guys who did not get into Harvard or Stanford?" It is usually either that they are social misfits or blew the admissions interview or a combo of both. So don't do that.

Your GMAT is fine, even if 10 basis points below 'average' in light of your GPA. For a banker/PE guy your extras are in-line. Just be sure you get the right recommenders, or that some recommender does not screw you, and don't say anything stupid on your application like you want an MBA to start a gay pizza parlor chain.

At Stanford, which has a smaller hole for A-types like you, it sometimes helps to have pull. To paraphrase George Orwell, all the piggy 'top' PE shops in New York and L.A. and Greenwich are equal. But to Stanford, some top piggy PE shops are more on top than others. HBS has favorites as well, but they have more room. If you really want to go to Stanford, find out if there is a Stanford guru at your firm and start working that angle.

Odds at non-H/S/W places are slam dunk IF you convince them you really want to come. Columbia puts guys like you on the waitlist often, unless you say that you have to stay in New York City because you live in a rent control apartment and your partner is getting exotic plastic surgery procedures only available at a New York Hospital. Or better yet, you are in the middle of those procedures, and they just happen to take three years. Attach X-rays to application.

Mr. C-Level

- 720 GMAT
- 172 LSAT
- 3.9 GPA
- Undergraduate degree in finance from 'new' PAC-12 public university
- Work experience includes four years in private banking/wealth management at a large regional commercial bank
- Extracurriculars include heavy involvement in the production of independent and local student films; three years teaching in a religious organization; also launched an ongoing media company
- "I hope to integrate marketing and financial knowledge (MBA), as well as legal expertise in entertainment rights and contracts (JD), to land a C-level position within an entertainment/media company"

Odds of Success:

Harvard Business School: 40% to 50%
Stanford: 30% to 40%
Wharton: 50+%
Berkeley: 60%
UCLA: 60% to 70%
Duke: 60+%
Columbia: 50+%
Yale: 50+%

Sandy's Analysis: Has your "Large Regional Commercial Bank" bank ever sent anyone to business school? Look, on the facts, getting into law school should be easy, since that is mostly a numbers game, and yours seem to add up. And law schools will buy your "Man-Friday-to-Irving-Thalberg" Wet Dream, but B-schools are not interested in applicants who dream about policing copyright infringers.

"C-level" as in your charming locution, "land a C-level position within an entertainment/media company" is not a term that should ever appear on an MBA application. "C-section?" Maybe, if you are describing pre-natal leadership traits so precocious that you demanded a stretch role after eight months. My point being, you need to reframe you goals for business school along the lines of leading a media company in the forefront of innovation, new modes of distribution, and new ways of storytelling (esp. new stories about victims, minorities).

You have a mildly offbeat past, coming from private banking at a regional commercial bank and then making Indy films? And then all you can say is that you want to be the guy at Paramount who stops trailers and mock-ups from unauthorized sites on YouTube, or in your own words, "as well as legal expertise in entertainment rights and contracts?" Sounds a bit schizo to me, as if they guy who made Capturing The Friedmans now wanted to join the marketing department of Save The Children.

Okay, let's just say no one told you the secret handshake, and smart fella that you are, you now got it. A lot will depend, for B-school, on what they think of your job and your bank, what extras are beyond the film stuff, what kind of support your recommenders can give you, and how well you, throughout the application, execute on what I just told you to do.

"Launched a successful and ongoing media/photography/film production company." Mazel Tov (Oh Linda!!!), but why do you need an MBA? That is what I am not seeing clearly enough here. I'm being tough on you because I've seen a lot of similar types get disappointing results. A plus for you could be if your movies actually dealt with B-school pet topics like victims, etc. And I don't mean hipster band kids who are victims of crack addiction.

Ms. CFO Wannabe

- 740 GMAT
- 3.1 GPA
- Undergraduate degree in finance, marketing and international business from a Big 10 school
- Work experience includes three years as a commercial lending analyst at large regional bank
- Extracurricular involvement as a college athlete who spent a semester abroad; held lots of leadership positions and volunteer experience with boys and girls' club-type programs teaching financial literacy
- First in family to go to grad school and first woman to complete undergraduate degree
- Goal: "Want an MBA to become CFO of a Fortune 500 company"
- 26-year-old white female

Odds of Success:

Wharton: 15%
Chicago: 30% to 35%
Northwestern: 30% to 35%
Duke: 30% 40%
NYU: 40+%
Berkeley: 25%

Sandy's Analysis: Lots to like and your story all fits together which is a plus. The low GPA and non-prestige job are your big drawbacks. Have you thought of what is called in this game, "developing an alternative transcript," which usually means taking several courses at local colleges, either over the summer or at night. In a pinch, you could take these courses online, although IMHO online courses are not valued as much. People usually take 'harder' courses like stats, accounting, calculus, microeconomics, etc., and if you already took those, try the next level up. (You seem smart enough).

The idea is to show the schools that you are serious, so serious, you are willing to go through this hassle of taking those classes. Well, that would be the idea for you, since you have an anchor GMAT score. For other applicants with both low GPA and low-ish GMAT scores, taking courses shows that you actually can do the work. Even with an alternative transcript of some kind, I'd say you'd be a reach at Wharton. Too many applicants like you with better GPA, more elite schooling, and better jobs with similar GMATs.

At Kellogg and Chicago, you could be in the hunt, since both of those places are open to your compelling personal story (athlete, extras, etc.) and your goals are a tight fit with your past. You might think about saying you are interested in regional banking as well, or just plain big banking. You have the background for it. Tuck would be a good reach as well. You're their type, totally. As noted here before, you need to rush them like a Sorority: visit, make friends, etc. Duke, Darden (which you don't mention) Cornell (also worth thinking about), NYU and Berkeley are worth applying to. An alternative transcript of two or four courses between now and when you apply would really help meet those places half way.

Mr. Portfolio

- 730 GMAT
- 3.76 GPA
- Undergraduate degree in economics
- Work experience includes six months at small financial services consulting firm; 1.5 years in sales and trading at an industry firm; and currently a portfolio management associate at a large firm.
- Extracurricular activity includes traveling a year in the Middle East and current board member of Pediatric Cancer Foundation
- Goal: To move up the ranks of portfolio management, build my network and finance skills"
- 25-year-old male

Odds of Success:

Harvard: 20%
Stanford: 10%
Wharton: 35%
Chicago: 40%
Northwestern: 35%
Columbia: 35%
MIT: 30%
Dartmouth: 30%
New York: 40%

Sandy's Analysis: Real solid stats, as noted many times. HBS and Stanford are not in love with Port Managers since they don't believe you need an MBA to do what your goal is, viz "move up in the ranks of portfolio management, build my network and finance skills."

That, plus two mildly grease ball early jobs (TO THEM) in sales and trading (might as well say "jails and hating") make you not their type. Pediatric Cancer Foundation is fine by me, but it won't wash you clean to them. Wharton is where guys like you wind up—portfolio management not two dirty words over there, and given solid stats, and all around good guy-ness, that is a real possibility.

Other top schools will fall into place so long as you don't run into an asset-management hater and also convince them of why you need the MBA. NYU and Columbia programs you mention should be totally in-line.

Mr. Corporate Development

- 720 GMAT
- 3.2 GPA
- Undergraduate degree in economics from Ivy League school
- Work experience includes two years at a bulge bracket investment bank (Lazard/ Credit Suisse/JP Morgan); worked in Latin America M&A team; and two years in corporate development for a large west coast consumer/retail company (Levi's/ Nike/Starbucks).
- Extracurricular involvement in minority business programs; led team of students in a consulting project for economic development; alumni interviewer for undergraduate school
- Goal: To work for a consumer/retail focused private equity fund
- 25-year-old Hispanic male and first-generation college student from South Central Los Angeles

Odds of Success:

Harvard: 35%
Stanford: 25%
Wharton: 35% to 40%
Berkeley: 50+%
Dartmouth: 30% to 35%
Yale: 35+%
Columbia: 35%

Sandy's Analysis: The 720 GMAT may help soften the 3.2 (as will the fact the 3.2 was in economics at an Ivy) and the Hispanic-South Central-Ivy personal story is solid. The move from IB to corporate development might be suspect to cynics (and adcoms are cynical) as representing a slower track, and such a move is unusual. The fact you seem to be at brand-name company is a plus.

Soooooo, in total, we got a good 'identity politics' story, a low-ish GPA, a good GMAT, a good first job, a maybe 2nd job, and real strong extras. Phew, hard to know how that all pours out of the cocktail shaker.

I'm not sure your saying you want to focus on consumer/retail private equity is the right goal. It sounds like you are trying to prove something to the guys back at the IB. You might do better saying you want to go into strategy consulting as a gateway to running such a company, or starting one focused on ethical trends in retail. The way guys like you get into Stanford is if your company has connections (calling Nike!!!!) and that tilts you over, e.g. a real powerful recommendation and maybe a phone call from someone who is a player at Stanford. That, plus solid execution. Guys like you get into and dinged at HBS based on execution, connections, luck, recommendations. Ditto Wharton, but that 3.2 may hurt you more there, they are picky about core numbers. Other schools you mention should be in range if convince them you want to come.

You're a volatile case, and could go either way, the real key for you is to somehow reposition the second job as an opportunity and not a come-down. In order to do that, you need to show that 2nd job is gateway to goals, and I don't mean 'retail' private equity. Execution for you really matters (e.g. more than for most people who have more simple stories to tell) because of the 3.2 and 2nd job, so we gotta wind up reading your app, and liking you, and understanding why experience so far, and projected goals, and extras, all support each other.

One unknown for applicants in Round One next year will be the "Romney-effect" on private equity (assuming Mitt is the candidate vs. Obama). My guess is private equity will always get a fair-to-mildly-pro-biased hearing in B- schools, but there will be a residue negative effect, viz, that many private equity wannabes (that is YOU) vs. seasoned practitioners, are just looking for a quick payday and a low tax rate.

That is part of the reason I advise strongly against saying private equity. That might be an OK thing for a current PE guy to say, but you are a wanna-be, and subtly, that changes everything.

Mr. Hedge Fund

- 750 GMAT
- 2.9 GPA
- Undergraduate degree in aerospace engineering from MIT
- Work experience includes four years as a trader at a quantitative hedge fund
- Extracurricular involvement is extensive with community service, mentoring underprivileged youth and performing arts
- Goal: "Management in renewable energy related manufacturing or R&D firm"
- "Applied Round 1 to HBS, GSB, MIT, Kellogg but have already been declined without interview from HBS."
- 24-year-old African-American male who was born in Cameroon, lived in France and moved to the U.S. at the age of 11

Odds of Success:

Harvard: -15%
Stanford: 10%
MIT: 25% to 50%
Kellogg: 35% to 50%

Sandy's Analysis: Hmmmmm, Harvard does not like traders at quant hedge funds, because, well they don't. The only Hedge Fund types HBS really likes are DONORS. They also see trading as something they can-not teach, something which does not require management or leadership skills. All that said, African-American males with 750 GMATs and an MIT degree, even one with a 2.9, could be attractive, so if you had been inter-viewed, I would not have been surprised. It was a worthwhile roll of the dice.

I hope you did a good job minimizing the 2.9, beyond saying you had a lot of extras and was distracted. What goes for HBS also goes for your chances at Stanford. They don't like traders either, or a 2.9, but could blink if they find the rest attractive. Let's face it, with a 750 GMAT, it's not like these places are taking much of a risk.

If you were able to cook up some story based around your interesting upbringing, well, you got an outside chance, although I think it's less than 15%. MIT might take you based on GMAT and the fact that "hedge fund" and "trader' are not dirty words over there, and they have a hard time recruiting African-American males. So chances there are in the 25% to 50% range. Kellogg might go for the 750 and the community service.

Not sure what I make of your goals: "Management in renewable energy related manufacturing or R&D firm." That seems to come out of no place. Here's a million dollars worth of advice. Find some big shot at your Hedge Fund who can make some phone calls for you–that is one way guys like you get into Stanford, and also MIT and Kellogg.

Does anyone at your firm know Andy Lo? He is the big Sloan School financial engineering honcho. If someone called him and said you were worth a look, that could really make a difference.

Really go through all your contacts, and their contacts, and try to get a phone call made on your behalf. Get your sales pitch together with more tailored goals to something you have done.

Mr. Junior Olympian

- 700 GMAT
- 3.6 GPA
- Undergraduate degree from a Rutgers University-type school, while running a multi-million business throughout college (family turmoil)
- Work experience as an investment banker in New York for three years, with a year-long stint in an operational role at a bulge bracket i-bank
- Extracurricular involvement as a three-time junior Olympian, captain of the junior Olympic team and a national champion athlete; also serve on the board of two non-profits for children
- 27-year-old South Asian U.S. citizen

Odds of Success:

Harvard: 10% to 15%
Wharton: 20+%
Chicago: 40+%
Kellogg: 40+%
Columbia: 30% to 50%

Sandy's Analysis: Hmmmm, a lot of silver here instead of gold, including Rutgers-type school, Junior Olympics and not Olympics, operational role at IB, and wrong type of minority (South Asian, which don't count for nada in adcom's eyes).

Don't get me wrong, I'm impressed with all that, having a good deal of silver, if not bronze and cooper (and lead) in my own life, but I am not applying to business school.

This ain't smelling like Harvard or Stanford, if that is your question, nor will super-duper extras help you at Wharton, where silver goes to nest, in

192

many cases. Guys like you are real solid at places like Chicago (where extras count), Kellogg and possibly Tuck.

But somehow I get a vibe that is not what you had in mind. I'm not sure what managing a multi-million dollar family business in college means, although I'll take the hint about family turmoil, but still? Anyway, that won't help as much as you might hope. It is too real. Given numbers and New York (if so) center of gravity, Columbia is a good choice. These stories fill out their application very well, and they like bankers, and you seem employable after graduation.

Mr. Inner City

- 650 GMAT
- 3.2 GPA from Ivy League school (not Harvard, Yale or Princeton)
- Undergraduate degree in economics
- First generation college student, Latino who grew up in Oakland
- Work experience includes a year in a "post-MBA job" in corporate mergers & acquisitions for a popular company in the Pacific Northwest (not Amazon or Microsoft); a year on investing side of a private equity "Mega Fund" in New York; two years at a "top-tier" bulge bracket investment bank
- Extracurricular activity in minority business programs and microfinance advocate at I-Bank

> **Odds of Success:**
>
> Stanford: 20% to 30%
> Harvard: 25% to 40%
> Wharton: 25% to 50%
> Yale: 40% to 60%
> Tuck: 40% to 60%
> Columbia: 30% to 60%
> Berkeley: 40% to 60%

Sandy's Analysis: Phew, let's summarize: 1) Latino; 2) 3.2 GPA and a 650 GMAT; 3) An interesting identity politics story, maybe, depending on what you make of growing up in Oakland, and 4) What seems like a career that has maybe one too many jobs which has gone from bulge bracket bank, where you say "top tiers" (love that plural, that could mean bottom of 2nd tier, e.g. 60%), to one year in Mega Fund (the actual status of that fund on the pecking order can be important), to the all important current job, at **XXXX** the very popular firm in Pacific NW, which you claim to have joined because of some amazing opportunity.

Let me give you the tough love first. That XXXX company better be Nike or Boeing or some other no-explanations-needed company, and your reasons for joining better be crystal clear and supported by recommendations because most hotshot PE kids don't walk away from the Bright Lights to become middle managers in a very rainy climate at a company which is not Microsoft or Amazon, or even at those companies.

Also, being in a so-called "post MBA" position, is not always good. It often means you stayed around too long and just got some cost-of-living promotion. The reason I am being so hard on you is because both your GPA and GMAT are super low for everything else on this record, so it just makes one wonder. And just some general advice, for anyone with a 650 GMAT, you always have to take it again, just to show them you care about the process and tried. You can't possibly write an essay about how the GMAT does not reflect your true abilities unless you have at least taken it twice.

The envelope please: Stanford (less than 20%) because they got Latino first gens like you with better stats and just as good inner city jive, unless your extras are really, really powerful and sustained. HBS (25% to 30%) with same thinking as Stanford, although they got more room, so you might sneak in. Wharton (25% to 30%), low grades and low standardized testing will spook them. Ditto Columbia, Yale, Tuck, and Berkeley which could be 40% to 60%.

Do you want to do yourself a favor, retake the GMAT and keep retaking it. Take if four more times, and get the highest score you can. No school cares about what the test means, they just want the number, and if you can get that up to 710+, your whole story gains a ton of credibility.

Mr. Triple Degree

- 710 GMAT
- 3.65 GPA
- Three undergraduate degrees in accounting/finance (3.85 GPA), mathematics (3.8 GPA) and art history (3.2 GPA) from a mid-tier state school
- Completed three degrees in four years, taking 22-24 credits a semester (at least 5 semesters)
- Work experience includes two years at bulge bracket investment bank in controller and risk management
- Extracurriculars include role as vice president in a business fraternity, leader for an "early career" church group
- "Looking to make a career switch to a more client-facing role such as consulting."
- 23-year-old Asian

Odds of Success:

Harvard Business School: -20%
MIT: 25%
Yale: 30%
Wharton: 25%
Tuck: 30%
Booth: 40%
Columbia: 40%
NYU: 40+%

Sandy's Analysis: Well, I like you and your hard work but this is not looking like an HBS profile. There are too many Chinese guys with similar stories and better schooling, stats, and jobs. And extras are weak as well, for HBS. I would say that goes for Wharton, too. The fact you have a non-client facing role in IB and are not a classic ' investment banking division (IBD) analyst' is a deal breaker for those schools. They trust the selection process of the banks and will fill their finance bucket from that well.

You got a real outside chance at MIT only because they are hard to predict, don't care about extras, may blink at lower verbal portions of stats and you could be their type. Columbia might take you on just the 710 GMAT and grades and fact you are in New York (I assume) and could probably get a job when you graduate (an important piece for them), if not the one you really want. Tuck has lots of banking connections, and you seem like a sweet guy, so maybe if you went up there and found a niche, that could happen. Ditto Booth and Yale.

Mr. First Generation

- 730 GMAT
- 3.94 GPA
- Undergraduate degree in finance/accounting from SUNY School
- Work experience includes two summer internships at a bulge bracket investment bank, an off-season internship at another I-Bank, and another off-season internship at a small private equity shop
- Extracurricular involvement includes being founder and president of a campus mentoring program, president of my business fraternity, peer advisor in undergraduate B-school office, and singing in an acapella group
- 22 years old

Odds of Success:

Harvard 2+2: 20% to 50% (depends on life story)
Stanford: 20% to 30%
Wharton: 20% (next year but very good in three years)
Chicago: 30% (and ditto about the future)
Northwestern: 30% (and ditto)
Yale: 30% (and ditto)
MIT: 30% (they could take you flat out)

Sandy's Analysis: As to HBS 2+2 and Stanford, there is good news and bad news. The bad news is that every job, every extra, everything is just banks and b-school premature ejaculation. SUNY is also no one's favorite school, and it just fits too neatly with this profile of a smart kid who somehow could not swing Michigan, Berkeley, UVA or Penn.

The good news is a good many extras and initiatives, even if many are business centric, and a 3.94 at a school not known to give away easy A's.

This is an acceptable profile for first generation college kid from a poor immigrant family. That would explain a lot, and if that is the case, that story needs to play a strong part in your application. If you do that, admission odds go up. But, if you are some kid whose dad is a dentist in the suburbs and your family was too cheap to send you to the University of Michigan or Berkeley or UVA and pay out-of-state rates, well, that is ugly. You also need to expand any extras, which are not business related.

Well, having been in an acapella group is a bit exciting, but that is no high scoring extra unless you do rap and perform for charities instead of singing "Down By The Old Mill Stream" in nursing homes.

As to getting in next year as a college senior applicant to schools without a 2+2 program? Wharton will say, to quote what Orson Welles said when he first glimpsed Elizabeth Taylor when she was a 10-year-old, "Remind me to be around when she grows up." Meaning, after you graduate and get a job in investment banking and then private equity and then apply to Wharton, you will get in.

As to chances at other schools, they will question why you just don't wait. You do not have the profile (entrepreneur) of a kid that schools take at age 22 with no full-time experience. Those schools may admit you, however, and suggest you defer admission for two years or so.

Once you have three or four years of work experience, your chances at HBS and Stanford are still iffy. There is nothing super pushing you in, but chances at other places are solid. If you want to change this, get a job at Goldman and then a Blackstone-quality PE shop, get ranked in the top bucket, and develop one signature extracurricular activity.

Soldiers & Officers

A few years ago, when the dean of Harvard Business School was a Mormon, the great admissions myth about the school was that if you were a McKinsey consultant, a Mormon or a Marine, you were golden. And if you could manage to be all three at once, you were an automatic admit.

Joking aside, Harvard and other top business schools like military applicants and many schools, including Chicago Booth and the University of Virginia's Darden School of Business, are offering more scholarship aid to attract them.

But at all schools, military students are a distinct minority. In Harvard's Class of 2011, for example, only 3% of the MBA candidates were from the military. An analysis by one member of the class showed that of the 31 students, 13 were from the Army, nine from the Navy, six from the Marine Corps, two from the Air Force and one from the Coast Guard. All 31 Harvard MBA candidates were male officers, with 23% from the U.S. Military Academy and 19% from the U.S. Naval Academy. While not an official count by Harvard, which does not disclose this information, it was as accurate as you can find.

We present a more varied lot of candidates among our profiles, including men and women, those in the Special Forces, a Green Beret, engineers, submariners, and even a civilian with work experience at the U.S. Department of Defense.

Mr. Green Beret

- 730 GMAT
- 3.63 GPA
- Undergraduate degree in finance from Ohio State
- Work experience includes seven years with the U.S. Army Special Forces, during which he served multiple Iraq deployments, leading more than 140 Iraqi special operation soldiers; also worked closely with Sheiks and tribal leaders to solve local problems; seven years of service due to job commitments including the multiple deployments
- Extracurricular involvement includes an internship with the Department of Finance in the state of Ohio
- Goal: Trying to change to get into investment banking

Odds of Success:

Harvard: 40% to 50%
Stanford: 30+%
Wharton: 50+%
Chicago: 50+%

Sandy's Analysis: As noted several times, and as amazing as it seems for military applicants, college grade point average really counts because adcoms are not experts at discerning what a great military career is versus an ordinary one, as they can by looking at a private employment record, where they have a better "feel" for the company you work for, and even how to read through your recommendations.

That being said, everyone {hearts} Special Forces, so that is an intangible plus. The work you did in Iraq, leading different types of resources in different ways, is totally up the alley of all adcoms, so tilt your essays in that direction. Other things they like to hear are some non-military stories

202

or semi-military stories about working with civilian groups, volunteering, and dealing with military families.

Your story – Special Forces, 3.6 GPA from an OK school, and a 730 GMAT – puts you in the running at H/S/W for sure. The eventual outcome will turn on execution, recommendations, and luck. Stanford may want to hear something a bit extra, e.g. overcoming adversity in terms of background, or some real do-gooder military stories. At HBS guys like you get in and dinged all the time, and guys like you usually get into Wharton, since they run older, and care most about your very solid GPA and GMAT.

This is a small point, but saying you want to go into investment banking, after this career, is a small let down. You might think about tweaking that a bit. Going commando on the battlefield is excellent; doing so on Wall Street is not an interesting story at this point in the financial cycle (to adcoms, it is to ME!!!!!!). Try spinning that into becoming an impact investor, especially in developing countries, maybe the Middle East, or some jive like that.

Pick you recommenders with care. Military officers who write grad school recs run from "outstanding" to disappointing. It helps to tutor them, if possible, at what schools are looking for– although the diplomacy of that is admittedly touchy. All top schools have Armed Forces clubs, which can be really helpful in explaining the secret handshakes which work better for recommendations, so reach out to them.

Mr. Army Engineer Officer

- 700 GMAT
- 2.9 GPA
- Undergraduate degree in electrical engineering from the University of Wisconsin
- 4.0 GPA
- Graduate degree in engineering management from Missouri University of Science and Technology
- Work experience as a U.S. Army Engineer Officer, Captain from 2005 to the present.. Deployed to Iraq in 2006-07 as an Infantry Platoon Leader, lots of great leadership stories. Selected above peers to take command of a company as a First Lieutenant (generally a Captain position). Work as an instructor at the Army Engineer School, honed leadership skills and developed solid mentoring and teaching skills. Deployed (currently) to Afghanistan as a long-range operations planning officer.
- Extracurricular: Led the community service project while in my Engineer Captains Course. I chaired the committee and led the execution of a 5k fun run fundraiser that had over 400 participants, 15 sponsors, and raised over $15,000 for the Wounded Warrior Project. Coached youth baseball for 4 years and volunteer occasionally with the boy scouts.
- Goal: "Looking to get in to I-banking and Sales/Trading or M&A. Long term, I just want to lead people."
- 32-year-old, married white male

Odds of Success:

Wharton: 35% to 40%
Chicago: 30% to 50%
MIT: 20% to 30%
Northwestern: 30+%
Dartmouth: 25+%
Virginia: 30% to 50%
Duke: 30% to 50%

Sandy's Analysis: Well, I like you and so might your target schools, but you are not a typical Army applicant because you're older (and not a pilot etc. where a long-term commitment prior to training makes you put in eight years, sorry if I am wrong) and because of your targeted interests in investment banking and finance. Some military wind up in IB and Sales and Trading but few state that so clearly as a career objective.

The recent course work with the 4.0 GPA will do a lot to get you some slack for low undergraduate grades, but that is still worth explaining in whatever way you can. Aside from your age and low GPA issues, there is a lot to like, including current deployment to Afghanistan (everyone pulls for guys in a conflict zone) and history of extracurrics and leadership awards.

As noted prior here, war stories max out to adcoms (at some high level, but they max out) so having non-war stories is a big plus. Chicago seems a great choice since they are open to finance types and applications which seem to have a lot of heart, however defined. Sloan is open to finance types but a bit tone deaf to "heart" and will be less impressed with war stories but might appreciate engineering background. They are also more concerned about metrics like a low GPA (even though a long time ago) and they might scrutinize your GMAT Quant score.

Wharton is between Chicago and Sloan, but open to older military. On the other hand, they are just more selective, but it could happen. Kellogg likes guys like you but your interests in IB are not directly up their alley, although they are not closed to it. Tuck also likes guys like you, and you could maybe charm your way in there, if you visited and made friends.

Try to find vets at all those schools. This is not that hard to do because there is usually an Armed Forces club of some kind, and they are often pretty engaged in helping current military, esp. officers currently deployed in combat zones.   So bottom line is that you are in play at all those places. Duke and Darden are both known to run older and like military. I think you'd stand a real good chance there.

You will be 35-36 by the time you graduate and 'start' your banking career, which is old for civilians but most banks are hyper-patriotic (you would be too, with all that bail-out money J). The banks may cut you some slack in that department but schools are very concerned about grads actually being employed after graduation, so if you can, explain how you plan to transition into banking or mention any buddies you know who have done so at your age, or allude to discussions with banker vets, etc. Military guys often do well in sales-and-trading, sort of the civilian equivalent of combat. So that is another plus in your favor.

Just FYI, although you did not ask, I'd say HBS and Stanford are marginal because of your age, low grades, Tier-3 schooling, and just being in the army for too long. They like their military cohort to put in five or six years and then get out (unless pilots) and be either service academy or ROTC at Tier 1 and 2 colleges. Not impossible, but H+S would be long shots.

Ms. Submariner

- 680 GMAT
- 3.2 GPA
- Undergraduate degree from the U.S. Naval Academy with a double major in economics and political science
- Work experience as a U.S. Navy officer, a graduate of the Navy's Officer Nuclear Power program and one of only 18 women to be the first in the history of the Navy to break into one of the last male-only fields in the country: submarining
- Extracurricular involvement includes two years on the varsity crew team; as a novice moved up to the 2V varsity boat and was part of the team that won the Patriot League Championships
- "I plan either starting or becoming involved in a charity organization focusing on improving children's education in the U.S. prior to applying. I also will likely have my real estate license prior to applying."
- 25-year-old female, first generation college graduate

Odds of Success:

Harvard: 30+% (if you get a 700 GMAT)
Stanford: 20% to 30%
Wharton: 40%
INSEAD: 60% to 70%

Sandy's Analysis: Yikes, there are not that many women service academy grads at Harvard, Stanford or Wharton, period, not to mention submariners. This guy, a military officer who runs the useful blog <u>Military To Business</u>, notes that by his chummy reckoning (he seems to know lots of current military at HBS), the HBS class of 2011 has 31 U.S. military members— all officers and ALL MALE (not sure how many are ROTC, or, ahem, battlefield promotions). Female service academy graduates have attended HBS in the past, but they are few and far between.

The submariner twist is a super added plus. Any Wharton or Stanford readers who know the military gender breakouts there, please check in.

All that said, I'd plan on taking the GMAT until you got a 700+, which is a useful marker at HBS. Dee Leopold, the HBS adcom head, has been overheard (and this was reported to me, so it is semi-reliable, semi-gossip intel) as saying anything beyond 700 does not move the needle much, but you know Dee. Or maybe you don't. That means if they otherwise like you, they won't blink at a 700. If you have a score below 700, well, they still may take you, but they will have to like you even more.

As I have noted many times about military applicants, GPA is one of the better predictors of admissions success, since the war stories all seem to bleach out, although recommendations are also important, given that powerful ones can cite where you stand in your officer peer group, which I understand the military does on some formalized basis, more formalized than, let's say, your bonus bucket at Ye Olde Generic Private Equity Shoppe. Your GPA of 3.2 is on the low side, so that is why I am suggesting a 700+ GMAT. Did you get 'grades' in the Nuclear Power Submarine Program? If they were better, it might be worth noting. That program, I am given to understand by grads, is a lot harder than regular Naval Academy fare, so that might also be worth noting.

As to what else you can do, starting/leading the charity you note focused on children's education would be a plus, as would any other non-military leadership gig. You note obtaining a real estate license? I mean, sure get one, but that is not any kind of plus to your application, and could be an odd downer.

So much else about your app will be fresh and unique, and the idea of being one of the buzzing bees of the real estate agent hive just seems to "normalize" you in a possibly disappointing way. Being a residential real estate agent, or even a commercial one, is not a gateway job to a Top 6 business school. Successful real estate agents can be very successful indeed, but there is no need for them to get an MBA. I strongly suggest, by the way, that you apply while still in the service. If somehow you thought getting out and selling real estate for two years would make your story stronger, well, it DEEPLY WILL NOT.

Mr. Platoon Leader

- 730 GMAT
- 3.8 GPA
- Undergraduate degree in mechanical engineering from the Royal Military College of Canada
- Work experience includes five years of continued leadership positions that include Afghanistan deployment as engineer team (platoon) leader.
- Extracurriculars are military-community sports, family events. Also includes some volunteering at special community events such as festivals. Essays/recommendations will include details as to why extracurriculars were hard to define given the military commitments.
- Goal: To continue move from tactical to strategic leadership in consulting post-MBA with eventual goal to start my own company that utilizes skill sets from military and MBA.
- First generation Chinese-Canadian, speaks English, French, Mandarin. Extensive travels with global mindset for future employment/ entrepreneurship.

Odds of Success:

Harvard: 45+%
Stanford: 30%
Wharton: 50+%

Sandy's Analysis: I'm pretty sure being Canadian military will not be a drawback, and might even be a plus, and if this were a West Point application with a 3.8 and a 730, and a cross-functional and cross-cultural Afghanistan deployment, I'd say your chances at HBS and Wharton would be pretty solid. Being first generation Chinese is an added plus. You don't need to explain why extracurriculars were military related. Schools understand that. Just have your recommenders do the usual rec things.

Work the volunteering at community events angle. Given solid grades and GMAT, and Chinese/Canadian twist, there is a lot to like here. As with many military applications, the trick is expand your accomplishments to include working with locales, working with enlisted guys who have marginal education, and initiating do-gooder stuff for villages, etc. Don't get caught up in "action-hero" stuff too much. Remember that by and large these applications are read by women. Stanford is always more selective, but you are in the chase there as well. A lot may turn on coming up with a stand-out "What matters most . . ." essay which somehow plays off first generation/Chinese themes and touches on what motivated you to attend the Royal Military College in first place. You can fill in "war stories" in the shorter essays.

Mr. Military

- 630 GMAT (second time, raised score from 500)
- 3.43 GPA
- Undergraduate degree in chemistry from the University of New Mexico
- Work experience includes six years as a captain in the Marine Corps; managed 200 personnel and $5 million of equipment; supervised a 39-man section and 50 Iraqi security personnel to provide protection and rebuild schools; also two years as an analytical chemist for a biotech company in San Diego
- Extracurricular involvement on the masters swim team, secretary of the American Chemical Society, three weeks building homes for under-privileged families in Mexico
- 32-year-old white male

Odds of Success:

Harvard: 10%
Stanford: 10%
Dartmouth: 20+%
Chicago: 20+%
Wharton: 20%
Duke: 30% to 50+%
NYU: 25%
UCLA: 25%

Sandy's Analysis: Are you in the military NOW?? ONCE AGAIN, PROFILE WRITERS, ALWAYS LABEL CURRENT JOB WITH THE LABEL, DUH, "CURRENT JOB" AND THEN LIST OTHERS IN REVERSE CHRONO.

If so, your chances are probably better than if you had spent six years in the military and then got a two-year chemistry gig at a biotech Company since your military experience is varied, impressive and full of leadership, business-type stuff, and consulting, even by military standards.

Schools are willing to blink at age for military applicants, and especially applicants, typically pilots, who are required to commit for eight+ years as part of the training.

If you left the military, got the job as a chemist with the biotech company, and now, two years later, have come to a B-school moment, that is probably less attractive, and schools might suggest you look into part-time or EMBA programs.

As noted many times, the dirty little secret with HBS (and Stanford) and the military is the surprising importance of the GPA (and also, a bit, the GMAT. Even years and many foreign scrapes later, the GPA still counts, and Harvard and Stanford (and other schools as well) trust it as a filter because they have a lot of experience with GPA and also much semi-bogus statistics.

Your GPA is a little low, and your current GMAT is way low. So Mission #1 for you is getting the GMAT to 680, or ideally 700, if you can. (Take it five times, no one cares, they just want to see the score.) You're a great guy with some dense and rich experience, but that will not overcome a low-ish GPA and a low GMAT.

I'm not seeing this as HBS or Stanford. There are just too many dents in the profile, e.g. age, lowish metrics, odd work stuff, whatever you are doing currently. H and S like military guys who are 1. service academy or ROTC and 2. who do their five-year gig, and who move on to B-school.

Your best chance on the medal stand is Wharton, which is real partial to military guys, even older ones, but Wharton is also the most GMAT focused of H/S/W, so you really need to jack up that score, if possible.

Tuck likes older guys as well, and you seem, at a quick look (which is often correct) to be their type: earnest, athletic, community-minded. Booth is a possibility as are other schools ranked third to tenth on PoetsandQuants because of reasons already stated. The classic schools for older, military applicants are Duke and Darden, and you would fit in very well there as well, so check 'em out.

If you are working for a biotech company now, sure, get that into your Goals/Mission/Why this school statement following advice to Marine Biologist in profile above. Biotech is sexy, but it not going to seduce HBS or Stanford in light of the irregularities of GPA, age, and military+job already vs. just military.

Mr. Submarine Officer

- 700 GMAT
- 3.45 GPA
- Undergraduate degree from the Naval Academy
- "After Annapolis, I went through the Navy's demanding nuclear pro-pulsion pipeline and became a submarine officer."
- Work experience includes stints as a reactor controls officer, a radio-logical controls officer and a tactical systems officer for 14 months on a submarine
- "I took the ship's radiological controls program from below average to above average in 8 months...I have the opportunity to get out in May or do a seven-month stint overseas as an operations officer in Bahrain"
- Grew up on a farm, one of nine children and only one to go to college
- Fluent in modern standard Arabic and conversational ability in German
- Goal: To use the MBA to get into the energy industry (would love to get into projects management)
- 28-year-old white male

Odds of Success:

Stanford: 20%
Harvard: 30% to 35%
MIT: 30%
Chicago: 40+%
Northwestern: 40+%

Sandy's Analysis: The dirty little secret about service academy grads and HBS (and a bit MIT) is that your GPA really counts (along with any GMAT 700+ which you have).

Amazingly, what counts after that is extracurriculars, which are hard to come by on a submarine. Let me explain for our military readers. War stories all tend to blend in the adcom's mind (but not mine!!! I love war stories, but then again, I'm not an adcom), but they expect some generic leadership blah, blah where you get to lead enlisted men. It doesn't much matter if that is in battle or in the engine room of a submarine. Going to Bahrain will not add much to your application, in my humble opinion. My really strong advice is to use any college or service related extra curriculars, as well as sure, a couple of sub stories.

Your 3.45 and 700 are both lowish for HBS, so I think you are going to have a hard time there. MIT might go for the nuclear stuff and solid record (they don't care about extra currics) and they like military but they like big GMATs more. You are in-line at Chicago and Kellogg and it is just a matter of solid execution. I ain't seeing this as Stanford. There's nothing driving you in. Growing up on a farm and being one of nine children is exotic, and will score well as a back story, so it's worth one HBS essay (Wish you had asked me about growing up on a farm with eight siblings, etc.) and can be used in other applications as well, obviously.

You might have gotten into Stanford if you grew up on a farm—as a slave.

Captain Military

- 620 GMAT
- 3.1 GPA
- Undergraduate degree in management and systems engineering from the U.S. Military Academy
- Work experience includes seven years of service in the U.S. Army as a captain who has done two combat tours. Commanded a company of 152 soldiers and served as deputy senior logistician in a unit of 2,700 soldiers. Currently a basic training instructor for newly commissioned officers
- Short-term goal is to work for a consulting firm with a federal practice in the defense sector. Long-term goal is to start a company that specializes in preparing enlisted soldiers who are about to transition from the military to the world of academia and earn their degrees. Picture a version of MLT for soldiers.
- "With the exception of Duke, I will be applying through the Consortium."
- 30-year-old African-American male

Odds of Success:

Dartmouth: 30%
Duke: 30% to 40%
Darden: 35% to 45%
Cornell: 35% to 50%
Michigan: 35% to 50%
UNC: 30% to 50%
Indiana: 30% to 50%

Sandy's Analysis: Well, I'm impressed with your service and leadership and the schools might be as well. What you might find, however, is that after the battlefield smoke clears, your GMAT and GPA remain. Schools are willing to blink at one, but both of yours are below average for those schools, although GPA only by a bit.

Obviously, there is lots to like in your profile and that may tip it. All those schools take applicants with each of your scores, and you could be a solid case to take a chance on. I'm not sure your goals—defense consulting and MLT for soldiers—are doing you as much good as you imagine.

The picture schools get is of a guy who cannot get his head out of the military and defense. You might just say strategic consulting, period, in order to apply skills you have learned in the military and help companies grow and add jobs. And say you want to be an impactful leader of companies, and you admire companies like General Electric and blah and blah for creating great products and jobs and helping communities.

Long term, your commitment to help enlisted guys transition from the military and earn degrees shouldn't be a business goal per se. You should make it a passion you will pursue in addition to industrial leadership. Possibly as well as part of working for a Fortune 500 company or major consulting shop.

I think your choice of schools is shrewd and it is just a matter of finding an adcom willing to blink about the 620 and 3.1. All of those schools do in some cases, and your case is pretty compelling.

Mr. Civilian

- 680 GMAT
- 3.4 GPA
- Undergraduate degree from a top private university
- 3.6 Graduate GPA
- Graduate degree from same school in finance
- Has been negotiating multi-million dollar defense contracts for the U.S. Department of Defense for two-plus years, with significant leadership experience
- Extracurricular activity involves leadership role in alumni organization and a volunteer at the National Gallery of Art and a local community center

---

Odds of Success:

Dartmouth: Less than 50%
Columbia: Less than 50%
Kellogg: 50%
Darden: 50+%
Duke: 50+%
Michigan: 50+%
NYU: 50% to 60%
Georgetown: 60%

Sandy's Analysis: This is all of a piece, with sorta okay school, but not Ivy or public Ivy, or apparently Williams (sorry if I am wrong because "top private university" can mean a lot of things), lowish GMAT and GPA, and a job which sounds on the low side of a good job—once again, issue is, how selective is that gig?

A good version of that same job, I think, is the Rotational Leadership Program at a major defense contractor: to wit, Raytheon, Lockheed, which are often big league gateways to eager beaver kids from second-tier colleges. Not sure if the Pentagon is exactly in that ring or next one out. Columbia is a good reach for you so I would try to apply early decision, but you will need to get a bit lucky. Your GPA and GMAT are just one standard deviation off for them (like I know what that means, but you get the idea), and this is not reading like a New York story. I'd say your chances at Kellogg are 30 to 50 percent, if you execute well, and sound Kellogg-y (which you do! given extras, and rah-rah Bowdoin/Bates/Scripps type college); Darden/Duke, hmmm you are on younger side there, if indeed you are two years out of college, but it all adds up; Michigan maybe; Georgetown takes kids like you; Tuck, see notes on "one standard deviation" off.

Mr. Navy

- 700 GMAT
- 3.25 GPA
- Undergraduate degree from the University of Washington in industrial engineering
- Naval officer for six years with intense, sometimes dangerous work experience, supervising personnel, managing complex projects and driving ships
- Extracurricular involvement includes two years as an after school reading and creative writing tutor
- Grew up in Europe (four countries in first 18 years), lived in Japan for two and one-half years
- Has a working knowledge of the Italian language

Odds of Success:

Harvard Business School: Less than 30%
Stanford: 20% to 30%
Wharton: Less than 50%
Dartmouth: 30% to 50%
Columbia: Less than 40%
Kellogg: 40% to 60%
Michigan: Better than 50%

Sandy's Analysis: The dirty secret about military admissions to places like Harvard/Stanford/Wharton is that GPA is a key factor and that war stories don't payoff as much as you think they should. Plus, lots of military applicants have shooting war stories these days as a result of ground deployments in Iraq and Afghanistan. The big payoffs for military applicants, as far as schools are concerned, is not work stories per se, but working with others, both enlisted personnel and locals. 'Helping my troops get along with the tribal leaders and setting up a school for girls, etc.' is a real solid HBS (and other schools) essay.

In your case, the deal breaker at Harvard and Stanford might be the GPA, assuming a solid GMAT (which we define here as 80 percent on both sides). The military career part seems in line and the extras are a plus. In general, schools are pre-disposed toward military candidates so you got a chance at non-H/S/W schools and a reach chance at Wharton. The international experience is nice, but it is not going to blow open any doors unless you can closely link it to your career goals.

Mr. Marine Captain

- 620 GMAT
- 3.0 GPA
- Undergraduate degree in geography from a public liberal arts university
- Captain in U.S. Marine Corps with two combat deployments in Afghanistan
- Nothing compelling in extracurricular involvement

> **Odds of Success:**
>
> Harvard Business School: Less than 10%
> Stanford: Less than 10%
> Wharton: Less than 30%
> Kellogg: Better than 30%
> Duke and Darden: Better than 50%

Sandy's Analysis: Well, Captain, I like you. But like I said to the Naval officer above, your low GPA will be a deal breaker for Harvard, Stanford and Wharton, and powerful combat deployments do not, without more, change the balance. And I suggest you format your combat experiences with suggestions above, ie. working with natives, leading different groups in different ways.

Also, if this report is an accurate reflection of your state of mind, you also need to start spinning this more and think about all the stuff you have done to help locals. A low GPA and a low GMAT is a tough nut to crack, so getting that GMAT score up will really help. If you have to take the exam five times, do it. This is not going to be a Harvard, Stanford, or Wharton admit. But guys like you are welcome at Duke, Darden, etc. Get a 680 GMAT and try those places. You'll love it, and they'll like you.

Mr. Special Forces

- 700 GMAT
- 2.5 GPA
- Undergraduate degree in systems engineering from West Point
- Currently in a leadership position in a Special Forces unit "given to a select type of individual" (first ever in U.S. Army history)
- Six of his seven years in the military have been in direct leadership positions
- Extracurricular involvement includes sports, one year volunteer at an orphanage
- Speaks two languages

Odds of Success:

Harvard Business School: 40+%
Wharton: 40% to 55%
MIT: Less than 40%
Chicago: Better than 50%
Columbia: Better than 50%
NYU: Better than 50%

Sandy's Analysis: As noted in the past, the dirty little secret about military admissions is how much the GPA counts, especially at Harvard Business School, since the Adcom folks there really don't have the skills or the desire to compare war stories. HBS does have a military guy on the Adcom, but that does not mean you will be interviewed by him, or that he will read your app.

HBS works under the laughing gas that everyone on the Adcom can read every app. While chicken hawk me is impressed with planning logistics for 3,000 Iraqi soldiers, it's just another deal to most Adcom members, although sure, 3,000 is a big number. What works more powerfully for military stories, just speaking in general now, is conflicts with locals, leading enlisted guys, leading foreign troops, and working with military families and children.

So all military applicants should think along those lines. The Special Forces angle is a wild card, given the big boost to Special Forces awareness in the Bin Laden aftermath. But sure, that is a plus, but it needs to be, ahem, "deployed" along with the same leadership lines as any other B-school story, with emphasis on leading diverse teams versus commando gung-ho stuff (send those stories to me!).

You will also need to explain why you have spent seven or eight years in service versus the usual five, and if that was a requirement of the Special Forces gig, or your choice. Schools have a varying awareness of military requirements for special roles, (pilots have to sign an eight-or-ten-year commitment to justify super-duper training).

As to your point in the bio—"currently in a leadership position given only to a select type of individual (first ever in U.S. Army history)—well, dunno. Obviously, that could be a game changer or a delusion. But if it is going to be a game changer, it has to be explained by a recommender as well as exploited by you.

Bottom line: I don't see extraordinary combat stuff overcoming low GPA and so-so GMAT overcoming low GPA at Harvard Business School, although I could be wrong if some of the X factors above turn out to be extraordinary on planet Adcom as well as on planet earth. Chances of admit there, assuming you do not get a personal recommendation and a 'must take' from General Petraeus, are 20 percent to 40 percent. At Wharton, where they like military guys and like older guys, your chances are 40 percent to 55 percent. MIT is not wild about soldiers per se, although they are happy to admit military who otherwise are in line with their admissions criteria. So odds there are less than 40 percent. Truth is, guys like you go to Duke and Darden, for sure, and sometimes break into HBS and Wharton depending on how your powerful intangibles play out.

The Non-Traditionalists

Non-traditional applicants come in many sizes and shapes. Typically, they're the people who apply to MBA programs who are not from traditional feeder industries or companies. They include military applicants (which we have chosen to define more clearly) and international MBA candidates who usually make up a third or more of the student population at most U.S. business schools (which we have also selected out for a special section).

Our group, profiled in the following pages, are an incredibly diverse lot, from a surgeon in his fourth year of specialty training to a pop recording artist whose music has charted in the top 50 in Japan and a National Football League (NFL) player.

Non-traditional candidates can be at a disadvantage in the race to get into a great business school. That's largely because they have little, if any, access to successful MBA candidates who can offer personal advice and counsel— and even a glimpse at a set of essays that helped get them into a Harvard or Stanford.

If you're consulting at McKinsey or in an investment banking job at Morgan Stanley, there are MBAs to the left and right of you and you probably report to one. If you're a non-traditional applicant, you're more likely to be surrounded by people who have never met a Harvard MBA.

Mr. Surgeon

- 730 GMAT
- 3.9 GPA
- Undergraduate degree in pre-med from the University of Toronto
- 3.7 GPA Med School
- Currently in fourth year of surgical specialty training
- Extracurricular involvement as a physician volunteer in an underdeveloped country and a couple of articles published in peer-reviewed journals
- Goal: Big dream to apply business models to public health care in order to increase efficiency or to start my own consulting firm
- 28-year-old Asian male, fluent in Cantonese

Odds of Success:

Harvard: 30% to 40+%
Stanford: 20% to 30%
Wharton: 50+%
MIT: 50+%

Sandy's Analysis: Come on down, Doc! That is a hunk-a, hunk-a powerful resume, and while no one loves surgeons as much as they love marine biologists, well, they do respect them. The trick of getting into HBS or Stanford for you will be selling your BIG goals in some specific and supported way. As noted, most docs at HBS are from Harvard or Yale medical school, or Harvard teaching hospitals, but Toronto has some classy cred in these parts that might serve as a substitute.

What you really need to do is get powerful docs and profs to support you and your goals. The one downside I see is that none of your many powerful pluses synch up with reforming health care delivery, and surgeons are not known for thinking big. They are known for big egos, which is a different matter. I might say you want to reform surgery instead of healthcare, in terms of delivery of services, especially in under-served areas, which could mean areas of Canada or the undeveloped world. That way your volunteer gig "adds up."

Becoming a consultant after all that training seems like a weak idea to me. You need to appear as a reformer and not a pre-mature burn out. Consulting would seem to throw away your surgical training. The docs I have known at HBS have used it as a career extender, not a blatant career change. You don't list schools, but what I said for HBS would also be true for Stanford, Wharton, and MIT. You can get a lot of guidance on this by checking out the Association of MD/MBA Degrees website—full of programs and developments.

Mr. Pop Star

- 740 GMAT
- 3.7 GPA
- Undergraduate degree in psychology from Yale
- Work experience includes four years as a pop recording artist signed to a major label with mainstream releases in Japan. Have singles charting in the top 50.
- Extracurricular involvement as the founder and president of a volunteer organization mentoring adoptees from other nations as well as extensive involvement in ethnic organizations
- Fluent in English, Japanese and Korean
- "I know I am a non-traditional applicant (I do not know of any other Japanese pop stars applying to b-school) but I have been planning on business school from the beginning. I had initially planned on lining up a job in management at a top Japanese record label (did a summer internship at a top label) but ended up signing to a label instead when they asked me to audition after seeing a demo tape that I sent. I thought that working in the industry as an artist would give me a unique vantage point for when I transitioned to the management side."
- Goal: "To return to Japan/Asia (the market is increasingly becoming pan-Asian) and hopefully be in a unique position to do top management work at a major label."

Odds of Success:

Harvard: 40+%
Stanford: 30% to 35+%
Wharton (Lauder Program): 40% to 60%
Columbia: 50+%
Chicago: 50+%
Dartmouth: 50+%

Sandy's Analysis: Sounds good to me, and you got all the bases covered, including a 3.7 from Yale and a 740 GMAT, plus solid extracurrics. You are not that much of a non-traditional candidate. Just stress, as you have in your note to us, your business intentions, and lay out some plausible career in media in Japan. You can say, as you propose, that you want to do 'management' at some record label, but try thinking bigger than that and say you want to build out your recording industry experiences to become a leader in digital media/new media blah, blah in Asia which could mean x y or z.

So much of music is now becoming morphed into other business models, e.g. Pandora or iTunes, etc. So lay out some possible futures using music and new media as a base, and for good measure, say you want to facilitate the exposure of new types of music, media, artists, art forms, although that is not strictly necessary. Truth is, Stanford loves jive like that, and HBS has been known to smile at it.

Ms. Hippie (with a touch of finance)

- 710 GMAT
- 3.4 GPA
- Undergraduate degree in finance from a top Canadian university
- Work experience includes one year at a global "now possibly imploded" hedge fund, a year and one-half in corporate finance for a "imploded" Icelandic Bank, and two years at a boutique media and entertainment financial advisory shop that is family-owned
- Have a full CFA
- Extracurricular involvement in student theater and broadcasting in college and now have a leadership role in a national arts education organization; also started a small digital film production company with my first feature film in production soon
- "Spent several months backpacking and supporting self through odd jobs on the road"
- Goal: To move into corporate development/strategic planning for a blue-chip media company
- 29-year-old woman who emigrated to Canada from an Eastern Bloc country at the age of 11

Odds of Success:

Harvard: 10%
Columbia: 20+%
NYU: 30%
UCLA: 30% to 50%
Berkeley: 30% to 40%
USC: 30% to 50+%

Sandy's Analysis: Are you employed now? A good deal of this will turn on that. If not, you come off as someone who cannot keep a job, despite the number of jobs you have had, and your resume tilts towards what you yourself call, "Hippie with a touch of finance." That is not a good handle for B-school.

On the other hand, if you are still working at the boutique media and advisory company, well, you are employed, if even at a 'boutique' in the field you want to wind up. It's a big difference. Note to those unhappy with your jobs: Don't quit until you get into B-school. I know, sometimes you get fired or the firm goes blotto.

Beyond that, what we got here is imploding hedge funds, imploding Icelandic banks, and almost-family media boutiques. This might make a good movie of some sort, "The Girl With the CFA Tattoo" but to turn it into a powerful business school application, I would actually cut back on the all the artsy stuff. The dirty little secret about business schools is that they hate artsy types, although they certainly welcome establishment ART types. How come? For the same reason everyone else does—too much attitude and hot air about creativity and too little accomplishment.

So, my advice to you, if not employed, is to not sound too liberated about it, but instead earnest about returning to employment. Similarly, I would not sound dismissive or fey about those other oddball 'imploding' jobs (well, I can be dismissive about them) and figure out instead how they could be a platform for current goals, how you learned x, y and z from them, even if that includes not wanting to do x and y.

The good news about you is that if you bleach out all the hippie-dippie-do stuff here we got a 3.4 in finance, a 710 GMAT, and some jobs that could be described as serious although, sure, not Tier 1. I think you got a good chance at Haas and UCLA if that is the way you presented yourself. It's so-so at NYU—they really hate 'artistes'— familiarity breeds contempt down there in the Village. I don't think you are getting in at Columbia because your stats are lowish and you seem relatively poor in terms of both family and job savings—this is a real issue for them.

USC, sure, just don't go artsy in the resume and app. Although the goals you state are fine.

Mr. Athletic Director

- 730 GMAT
- 3.2 GPA
- Undergraduate degree from the University of Michigan
- 3.8 Master's GPA
- Graduate degree in education from the University of Miami
- Work experience includes a two-year stint with Teach for America where I held leadership positions and created my own social change program to help students; now assistant operations manager for a national limo company.
- Extracurricular involvement as captain of the Michigan volleyball team but have also done a lot of volunteer work
- Goal: To combine my passions of sports and education to become an athletic director of a major university
- "I want my MBA in order to grow my leadership skills as well as enhance my knowledge of the financial and managerial aspects of being an A.D."

Odds of Success:

Northwestern: 10% to 20%
Stanford: 10%
Berkeley: 20%
Texas: 30% to 50%
Yale: 20%
UCLA: 30% to 40%
USC: 30% to 50%

Sandy's Analysis: Hmmmm, here's a question for you—

1. Teach for America
2. Limo company
3. College Athletic Director
4. Masters in Education

Which one does not fit? Well, maybe I am just being snarky and superficial because if you were an assistant manager for Zipcar, well, folks would think that is a hip and respectable job. And rest assured, both the assistant manager for Zipcar and assistant manager for a National Limo Service probably do pretty much the same thing.

A few words of advice: If possible, avoid the word "limo" in your application unless it is actually in the legal name of the company. Just say you work for a chartered car service or livery service. Surely, I am not the first to tell you this.

O.K. as to using all those degrees to become an Athletic Director at a major university, here you got me? For our international readers, <u>Athletic Directors</u> (often known as AD's) at major US universities are nominally in charge of all coaches, teams, etc., which at major sports schools can be a multi-million dollar set of enterprises with myriad responsibilities. Some head coaches, who are sometimes the AD as well, and some AD's, make millions of dollars per year and are often one of the most highly compensated people at the school, often earning more than the president—with good reason. Sounds like you could use an MBA, so the idea is not nuts. But someone tell me if any current AD's have MBA's? Or what degrees they do have?

All that said, I don't think you are getting into Stanford, whose own AD, Bob Bowsley, earned his bachelors degree from Minnesota State-Moorhead in 1975 and his master's degree from the University of Iowa in 1978.

But back to you, you are not getting into Stanford because your GPA is too low and because of the limo company, or whatever name you choose to call it, isn't the kind of work experience Stanford loves to see on a resume. It just does not compute for them, and while I am just guessing here, I don't think Derrick Bolton, who is the Stanford Business School AD (Admissions Director) is a super jock. Someone correct me if I am wrong, but don't correct me just based on the fact that Bolton is friendly with jocks. He is friendly with everyone. USC and UCLA, also iconic sports powers, may go for this story, and stats are not deal breakers there. This is not smelling like Kellogg or Yale, but, hey we are in unchartered territory. Berkeley is a coin flip.

You might think of expanding your goals to something more traditional such as sports management, a goal where the limo company experience begins to make oddball sense. The AD goal statement is risky. How many Division 1 AD's are there? It is over-specific, although I understand you want to play the education card as well. I would ponder your goals deeply, in many cookie-cutter cases, actual goals do not count, but in your case, an odd, wet dreamy, and rare goal such as D-1 AD could be a sign that you are not really interested in business and more interested in taking limo rides with rich alums.

Mr. Architect

- 710 GMAT
- 3.4 GPA
- Undergraduate and master's degree in architecture from an Ivy League university
- Work experience includes two years at a global architecture firm headquartered in New York, working on large-scale, mixed-use commercial developments throughout Asia; two years at a boutique architecture/development firm in New York. Also held four different teaching fellowships while a grad student. Currently starting a real estate development firm
- Goal: "After graduation, would hope to work at a REIT or PE real estate fund."
- 28-year-old Hispanic male and first-generation college graduate

---

Odds of Success:

Harvard: 40+%
Stanford: 20% to 30%
Wharton: 50%
Tuck: 40% to 60+%

Sandy's Analysis: Let me start with a nutty question: What was your graduate school GPA? Amazingly, it's not super important, but more important than you probably think, given your low-ish (for HBS and Stanford) undergraduate GPA of 3.4.

Aside from that, you are real solid: first-generation college, Hispanic, male, 710 GMAT, and your goals are not that off the grid. Most MBA programs, especially large ones, have dudes transitioning from a real estate base (including engineering, construction, and architecture) into development— and of all the possible real estate origins, well, everyone loves architects.

How come? Might be the relative rarity, the cool clothes, taking notes on graph paper, some <u>Fountainhead</u> holdover (for Tea Party fans), or whatever—well, we won't settle for whatever, check out <u>this</u> article at the "definitive" (in the muddled world of pop-culture criticism) Nerve website, Romancing About Architecture, Why the architect is Hollywood's go-to male love interest. Let's see, as the article notes, we got Joseph Gordon in 500 Days of Summer, Sam Waterston in Hannah and Her Sisters, Steve Martin in It's Complicated, Tom Hanks in Sleepless in Seattle and if all that is too white-bread for you, at the same website, not that I really looked, but check out the hot picture of Wesley Snipes in Jungle Fever, surveying Annabella Sciorra, on his drafting table, with those cool 'springy-grasshopper' architectural lamps framing the scene.

OK, I could go on, but the issue is will adcoms, in the full light of day, fall for architects like you the same way popcorn-popping, Rom-Com addled young women do in the dark?

I don't see why not. The fact that you work for a "global" architecture firm, headquartered in New York, man, those adcom chicks are getting weak in the knees already.

"After graduation, would hope to work at a REIT or PE real estate fund." Ok, that's a bummer, even without the Newt Gingrich attack ads on vulture capitalism. What the world does not need is one less dreamboat architect and one more dickhead REIT toad. Or so the prevailing wisdom is on Planet Adcom. You should really say you want to lead a development firm that focuses on the usual blah, blah . . . sustainable development, fusion architecture (I just made that up, but I'm sure it exists, where food leads, buildings soon follow, and it builds out on your Asian experience), mixed-use stuff with rich people, poor people, and a suburban Little League team, just like Trophy Projects x y and z.

Given how solid everything else is, I'd say you got some pretty good odds at HBS, Stanford, Wharton and Tuck. It all fits together as a story and a career, and you're an architect!

Mr. Football

- 700+ GMAT (studying now and hopes to land a 700+)
- 3.9 GPA
- Undergraduate degree in business management with a minor in accounting
- Work experience includes six years of playing in the NFL. He and his wife have also started a small business—women's fitness studio–that has been up and running for 18 months. "I feel my work experience has taught me a lot about leadership and teamwork."
- Extracurricular activity focused on football
- Goals: "Ultimately I am not sure what exactly I want to do post MBA. Does this hurt me? I have an idea based on what interests me now but will be open-minded as I go through grad school. But I feel an MBA is a great way to bridge the gap between football and the real world."
- Concerns: "Because of the timing with deadlines and our current season, I will be forced to apply to round three for all my schools. Does this eliminate my chances of getting into a Top 10 program? I have my eyes set on Stanford but would love to know if this is realistic."

Odds of Success:

Stanford: 50%+
Harvard: 50%+
Wharton: 60%+

Sandy's Analysis: Well, a 3.9 and an NFL career, and any kind of ~700 GMAT would put you in solid contention for Stanford and HBS and Wharton, even in the third round.

Schools love stories like yours since it supports the myth of their own diversity and openness to any background. Plus the solid stats make it risk free for them. Also, many adcoms are jock sniffers, although I am not drawing any straight or dotted lines to the peeps at H/S/W.

As to goals, just say you are interested in leadership, and that could be in sports or business. You want to have an impact: create opportunities for others. Stanford, or Wharton or HBS will help you become a general manager (that is key term) and also help you learn different leadership styles. The fact that you have started a small business is not as critical as you think, although sure you can mention it.

It might help to locate role models with athletic backgrounds who have become business leaders, although not many come to mind. Maybe our readers can help. Wikipedia says that Greg Comella, an NFL veteran, studied for an MBA at HBS, not clear if he graduated or what he is doing.

But you don't need to find athletes with MBA's per se, you just need to find athletes who have used their leadership and team skills to become successful in business and say that is what you want to do. You'd be a natural to start as a consultant and then join a growing or established company as one path, or use that base to start your own firm.

Oddly, The Harvard Crimson yesterday (Nov. 3) has a story about Clifton Dawson, an NFL veteran (Colts, Bengals and Houston Texans) who is now at HBS. The full story is worth a look. He is majoring in general management, and he also coached his section in flag football. You might drop him a line.

As to the third round, don't sweat it, dude. If you got a 3.9 and an NFL career and a ~700 GMAT, you chances of getting in are real, real solid.

They will find a place for you in Round Three.

Ms. Sorority

- 720 GMAT
- 3.2 GPA
- Undergraduate degrees in microbiology and the history of art from a Big 10 university (some C grades on transcript)
- Work experience includes three years working in the food industry and a short stint in clinical research understanding children's inner ear infections,
- Extracurricular involvement on board of directors for a non-profit throughout college, student government senator, sorority chair, active fundraiser and volunteer for various political organizations and non-profits
- 25-year-old female, who is 1/4 Hispanic and would be first-generation to go to grad school

---

Odds of Success:

Kellogg: 30+%
NYU: 30%
Chicago: 30+%
Georgetown: 40% to 50%
Virginia: 40%
Texas-Austin: 50%
Michigan: 50%

Sandy's Analysis: I'm not seeing this at Kellogg or Chicago, everything is too confused and low grades are the final straw, unless you can somehow put what you say is "three years working in the food industry" into some career path, or combine it with what seem to be strong extras (again, not specified). What does 'work in food industry' mean exactly?

Don't tell me, just a suggestion to other kids who want their profiles done, the less I know, the less good my advice is. I don't think the 1/4 Hispanic is going to open any doors either, unless you have a Hispanic surname, and maybe some connections to Hispanic community groups. What schools care about more than actual diversity is the government form they have to fill out which list the number of minorities by type, and Hispanic surname one type (along with lives in Puerto Rico), along with Native American, African-American. I don't know what happens if you are 9/10 Hispanic if your last name just happens to be O'Brien.

Darden just might bite here, if you get your story and motives straight, although I'd say odds there are 40 percent and sinking. Phew, I'm not sure this makes much sense at NYU because if they want to swallow a 3.2 GPA they may find a more tasty version than facts we see above, which, could be a lot better than your post. UT, GT, Michigan all take seriously packaged versions of you, so my parting words are SERIOUSLY PACKAGE yourself, we just don't see any motive for B-school in the above.

I could upgrade your chances everywhere if current job is serious, such as marketing at Nabisco, and you have goals, which directly emerge from that experience.

Mr. Tech Startup

- 720 GMAT
- 3.45 GPA
- Undergraduate degree in accounting/finance from a good school on the scale of Georgia Tech
- Work experience at U.S. Department of Commerce for three years, first in the Leadership Rotational Program, then permanently assigned to work on early stage tech projects and investments
- Interned twice and got a full-time offer from a bulge bracker investment banking firm but turned offer down because I became disillusioned with banking culture
- Recently launched tech startup that is a blend of Groupon and social media
- Extracurriculars include volunteer on local and national political campaigns, tutor inner city kids, and fundraising events for nonprofits.
- Fluent in five widely useful languages
- Future Goal: To become successful in business and use leadership experience to help formulate good business policies through special public service appointments.

> **Odds of Success:**
>
> Harvard Business School: 20%
> Stanford: 10%
> Columbia: 40%
> Wharton: 50%
> NYU: 60+%
> Yale: 60+%
> Georgetown: 70+%

Sandy's Analysis: I am assuming you are still with the Dept of Commerce and have not quit to work on start-up full-time. If you have quit, that is not good. Business schools despise entrepreneurs, especially ones at no-metrics, no VC-money, no professional websites, because anyone can be an entrepreneur and they have no way of knowing how to judge you. It helps if you have venture capital backing and revenues, but then, duh, why apply? As Mark Zuckerberg recently noted, he is seeking the best Harvard degree, honorary.

To business schools, entrepreneurs=burn outs with laptops. If you do strike gold, as per Mr. Zuckerberg, the school will be happy to become reacquainted over a cozy cashier's check. Okay, assuming you are still at Commerce Department, here is the low down on U.S. Government jobs.

How hard is that job to get, how many kids from your department applied to business school and what outcomes did they have? I'm no expert, but the last time I looked, the Tea Party wanted to abolish the Department of Commerce and no one else was too excited about it.

If you were admitted into some selective leadership rotational program, as you say you were, that could help. But most government admits to H and S, especially for white boys (as I assume you are) come from the Treasury, the White House, and maybe the Justice Department. Anyway, that is my feel for it. If someone has data or inside-the-beltway anecdotes, please share. You got a reach chance at Wharton because of a quanty 720, the fact that you're a bit older and they may put one finger up their nostril with the 3.45. If not, do a full nose hold. Same with Columbia, although just always a bit more easy. Yale, Georgetown and NYU, should be admits.

All that said, if you totally turned yourself into a diving bomb, and executed super-duper, and got lucky and had backing from some impressive sounding under-secretary, I could see Wharton. Somehow you just smell their type.

Ms. Washington, D.C.

- 700 GMAT
- 3.55 GPA
- Undergraduate degree from a public Ivy
- Work experience includes a year in local/state government, having worked on a state representative campaign and then in the legislative office of the rep; a year and one-half in a non-profit think tank for progressive policy issues; a year and one-half at the White House, and a year and counting at the Department of the Treasury
- Extracurricular activity includes having been a board member of Students for Choice and co-chair of Women's Issues Commission. Have since volunteered on various campaigns, Habitat for Humanity, and local soup kitchens
- Interested in non-profit and public sector management
- 27-year-old Hispanic/white female

Odds of Success:

Harvard Business School: 20% to 50% (but only near 50 if some bigfoot goes to bat for you)
Berkeley: 40% to 50%
Yale: 50+%
Duke: 60+%
Michigan: 60% to 70%
Virginia: 60+%

Sandy's Analysis: How Hispanic are you? Do you have a Hispanic surname and connections to Latin community, and especially do you have a Hispanic surname?

Hmmmmmm, what did you do at White House and Treasury? As noted, those are feeder government spots to Harvard and Stanford, and as noted, a lot will depend on how hard those jobs were to get, and who your peers were, and what you did. At HBS, kids like you get in and get dinged depending on how well they can put all those intangibles together and who they can juice for recommendations and phone calls.

If you can get some bold name at the White House or Treasury (does not have to be Obama but someone most of us have heard of) to really get behind your application, that can drive you into HBS since the rest is passable. That person has to do more than just write a recommendation; that person needs to make contact with someone at HBS and say, "Hey, real star here..............give her a look."

I just don't see you having any trouble at other schools you note. You are close enough to their average stats, you are some kind of Hispanic, you are female, you got some solid extras, and have better and more interesting work experience than they will see from 95% of their other applicants. Plus, it all fits, even though four jobs is a lot, in your case it makes sense.

Ms. West African Exporter

- 680 to 700 GMAT
- 3.96 GPA
- Undergraduate degree in political science and philosophy at an average university
- Work experience includes two years as a Peace Corps volunteer in a rural village in West Africa and one year with a USAID project in the West African handicraft sector. Developing a business plan to export products to the U.S.
- Fluent in French and proficient in local language (Bambara).
- Taking the GMAT in August: expecting a 680-700
- "I'm not your average B-school candidate and am interested to know whether my unique experiences are an advantage at the top schools."

Odds of Success:

Harvard Business School: 30% to 50%
Stanford: 15% to 35%
Berkeley: 50+%
Columbia: 40% to 60% (depends on GMAT)
NYU: 60% to 70% (just convince them you want to go)
Georgetown: 60% to 70% (just convince them you want to go)

Sandy's Analysis: You say: ""I'm not your average B-school candidate and am interested to know whether my unique experiences are an advantage at the top schools."

I say: Just remember the two dirty little secrets about 100 percent do-gooder types, e.g. Teach For America or Peace Corps types who have ONLY worked for those organizations and versus some dude who did two years at Goldman and then a year in the Peace Corps

1. GPA really counts, even if from an average school, and believe me a 3.96 from Flyover State U is way better than a 3.1 from Public Ivy, or even real Ivy. But also GMAT or GRE also counts. A 680-700 is marginal. Schools may blink depending on course work (your majors were Polical Science and Philosophy, I smell guts) and other factors.

2. The Do-Gooder Organization also counts, especially selectivity. How hard is it to get those jobs? Teach For America jobs are really selective and schools respect that filtering process, I am not sure Peace Corp scores as high as TFA but it is respected. USAID is probably in the middle, although someone correct me if I am wrong.

You say: "Developing a business plan to export West African products to the U.S."

I say: Forget that. You don't need an MBA and who cares anyway. The world is awash with ethnic products (I am assuming you are not exporting oil or rare earth minerals) and what you need to say is that you want to continue to be a leader in the NGO world, possibly at the World Bank, blah, blah, blah. Or manage charter schools or private schools in regions 1, 2, 3, etc.

That could be real important because given your lack of top-tier schooling and so-so selective do-gooder organizations, you have some residual flakiness in your profile. So you need to present yourself as a gung-ho future leader, not someone interested in setting up an export tchotchke business (Tchotchke? Look it up, or Ask Linda on Accepted.com, the den mother of the Jewish consultants and resident Yiddish expert).

Nota Bene: I will stick to my guns about your need to present more corporate do-gooder goals versus exporting bric-a-brac, especially given your background. Even after someone sends me the website of http://www.shokay.com, the winner of the HBS social enterprise contest in the mid-'90s and now a wonderful business which sells scarves, blankets, mittens and hats made from yak hair originating in Yunnan, China. Believe me, the kids who started that company did not say that was their goal. (Actually, they were at the Kennedy School and then picked up some HBS ringers when they entered the business plan contest.)

Ms. Do-Gooder

- 700 GMAT
- 3.4 GPA
- Undergraduate degree from Wellesley in economics and philosophy
- Work experience as an innovation analyst in IT department of a large healthcare organization for three years; social media marketing and program management at two social enterprises
- Extracurricular involvement as a volunteer in college who won a community service award; but nothing formal since then
- Pacific Islander female
- Any suggestions for a good fit?

Odds of Success:

Harvard Business School: Less than 20%
Stanford: Less than 15%
MIT Sloan: 30%
Berkeley: 20%
Wharton: 30%
Columbia: 30%

Sandy's Analysis: I am assuming you are not a U.S. citizen? If so, for example Samoan, your chances as a minority go up, possibly a lot. For the n-tenth time, 'minorities' for B-school applications means U.S. citizens who are African-Americans, Alaskan natives, American Indians or Native Americans, Asian Americans, Latino/as, Chicano/as, and Pacific Islanders. If you are from some undeserved place but are not a U.S. citizen that is good. But the school is not boosting its official U.S. minority stats by taking you.

Do we have five years of work experience here? Three years of IT at some health care organization and then two one-year gigs at social enterprises? Dunno. A lot depends on how serious/large/well-established those social enterprises are. If they are sketchy, your whole app can begin to sound odd and fragile. That is beginning to sound flakey, and potential burn out alerts, and a lot will depend on how solid those organizations are. Schools like Wellesley are solid, although your grades are low. Still, your GMAT is solid.

You are not getting into Harvard or Stanford. There's just not enough gold dust (defined as various factors which really set you apart) unless you can somehow concoct some story about how all this translates into improving health care delivery in the Pacific Islands.

Chances at Sloan? They are open to oddballs and if your GMAT quant score is high, they could use a person like you to counter their nerd image (and often admit them). Wharton seems less likely. Just nothing here they really need and stats —GPA and GMAT—are lowish for them. Haas, sure, if you convince them you want to come, and Columbia is a close one. Apply early decision and make a great case for how being in New York will help you learn about cutting edge health care delivery for when you get back to the Pacific Islands. I also think you're a likely 'fit' for Kellogg and Yale. They tend to love poets with social enterprise experience.

The Globalists

One of the unquestioned great benefits of a top quality MBA program is that it brings you into contact with an amazingly broad range of people, especially those from all over the world. Some 68 different countries are represented in Harvard Business School's Class of 2013.

But the competition to get into a top U.S. business school is particularly fierce among two of the fastest growing applicant pools in the world: China and India. Put simply, U.S. schools are overwhelmed with Chinese and Indian applicants. The result: acceptance rates for U.S. citizens can be four to five times higher than the rate of acceptance for applicants from China or India.

At some prominent business schools, international applicants now outnumber those from the U.S. That's the case at MIT Sloan, Duke University's Fuqua School, and Michigan's Ross School of Business. At Purdue University's Krannert School nearly eight out of ten in its MBA applicant pool in 2011 were international. At Washington University's Olin School of Business, 70% of its 2011 applicants to the full-time MBA program were non-U.S.

Yet, at all of these prestige B-schools the percentage of international students who are admitted and enrolled fall far behind the percentage who apply. At Washington's Olin School, for example, only 35% of the latest entering class is international—even though international candidates made up 70% of the school's applicant pool. Although 53% of the 3,452 applicants to Fuqua's full-time MBA program were international, only 30% of the students in this fall's entering class are not from the U.S.

International applicants from other parts of the world don't face higher hurdle rates because there aren't as many of them. In any case, on the following pages, we present a very diverse mix of applicants from all corners of the globe and Sandy's best advice to them.

Mr. International

- 720 GMAT (77% Quant)
- 3.4 GPA
- Undergraduate degree in engineering from a German university
- 3.14 Master's GPA
- Graduate degree in engineering from an Ivy League school in the U.S. (drop in GPA due to culture shock)
- Work experience includes two years at a top-tier U.S. bank, initially in IT followed by working as a quant on the trading desk for four years in New York and London
- Extracurricular involvement as a board member of the alumni association of my undergraduate university
- Applied to Wharton R2 for class of '13 and was rejected after being put on the summer waitlist.
- Goal: To become chief operating officer at a top financial services firm or to start my own firm supplying risk analytics
- 27-year-old Indian with vast international experience having studied in India, Germany, Australia and the U.S.

Odds of Success:

Wharton: 30% to 35+%
Stanford: 10%
Harvard: 10%
Chicago: 30+%
MIT: 30%
Northwestern: 30+%
Columbia: 25%

Sandy's Analysis: You don't need any help from me. It is all here. You got on Wharton's summer waitlist doing what you did last year. Just apply there again, and apply to schools, which are less selective. In your case, that could include MIT, since they like quants, although not quants with a 77% Quant on their GMATs. Columbia might be hard for stat reasons as well, although you fit their finance profile.

My advice this past summer would have been Columbia Early Decision. That would have maxed out your chances for a Top-5 school. You are not getting in to Stanford or HBS, for reasons you note, although not age per se. It's the six to seven years experience in finance IT and trading they don't like. The traders who get into H and S usually have solid-gold pedigrees in terms of schooling, stats, and GMATs.

I think Wharton is going to be hard, nothing seems improved. At any rate, when you apply there again, try to come up with improvements. Booth and Kellogg should be doable.

Mr. Cricket

- 720 GMAT
- 3.8 GPA
- Undergraduate degree from an unknown college in India
- Post-graduate diploma in management from a well-known program in India
- Have designation as a CFA, FRM (Financial Risk Manager), and a level one CAIA (Certified Alternative Investment Analyst)
- Work experience includes nine months as a senior research analysis at an S&P subsidiary in India, two years as a financial analyst for a boutique private equity firm in Abu Dhabi, and a year and one-half as a portfolio analyst for a well-known family office in Abu Dhabi
- Extracurricular involvement as captain of the cricket team at college, treasurer of the CFA Emirates and a member of the Red Crescent
- Reason for MBA: To "reach the next level, faster career progress, networking, change of location"
- 28-year-old Indian male

Odds of Success:

Harvard: -10%
Stanford: -10%
Wharton: -20%
Chicago: -20%
Columbia: -20%
NYU: -20%
INSEAD: 30% to 50%
London Business School: 30% to 50%

Sandy's Analysis: Your problem is not enough Blue Chip anything: schooling or work. Your jobs are all at small and unknown (to most B-schools) places and if you add to that a no-name college, it begins to set a pattern. The longish list of CFA, FRM, CAIA, and PGDM also begins to work against you in an odd and maybe unfair way. You seem pretty well grooved in what you are currently doing, so much so, that you have gotten all those certifications.

Why should a leading B-school think you need one more? I would also do better than this litany for why the MBA: "Reach the next level, faster career progress, Networking, Change of location." I mean I totally understand, but it just adds to the 'narrative' that you are a frustrated "lifer" analyst who WANTS TO BE A HAPPIER ANALYST IN A DIFFERENT CITY.

Most top business schools do not consider relocating you to a more fun city as part of their mission statement. So, Harvard, Stanford, and Wharton are not going to bite. Booth, Columbia, NYU might if you put some real zip into your motives for the MBA, given that your background is solid and mildly exotic. INSEAD and LBS are not all that hard to get into, especially LBS. And you seem their age and background. INSEAD might find all this a bit boring, so that might be an issue there.

Hire a consultant (not me), seriously. Nothing personal. I just don't focus on the schools you should focus on, but any competent consultant could help you standardize this package into something more attractive than your self-presentation above.

Mr. Financial Planning

- 640 GMAT, 112 TOEFL
- Graduated in top 1% of my class
- Undergraduate degree in business administration from Universitat Pompeu Fabra and Autonoma de Barcelona
- Work experience includes one year in General Electric's finance management program and three years as a financial planning and analysis manager in Spain and one-plus years in Denmark for a major European food company
- Extracurriculars include teaching a finance elective at a university in Spain for on-finance majors.
- Fluent in English, Spanish and Catalan with a good working knowledge of French
- Goal: To get into strategy consulting at McKinsey, Bain or BCG
- 28-year-old Spaniard

Odds of Success:

Harvard: 20% to 30%
Wharton: 30% to 40%
Stanford: 10%
Dartmouth: 30% to 50%
Northwestern: 30% to 60%
INSEAD: 30% to 50%
IMD: 30% to 50%
Oxford: 30% to 50+%
Cambridge: 30% to 50+%

Sandy's Analysis: Some tough love right off the bat: McKinsey (and I think Bain and BCG) request your GMAT scores and they look for 720 or 700 (depends who you ask) as sort of a minimum. They may make exceptions for people with your language skills and geographic expertise, but that is worth looking into. A 640 would be a deal breaker for McKinsey and I suspect Bain and BCG. If any readers have more intel on this issue, please post.

Aside from that, what we got are good grades, low-side TOEFL (112) and mixed work history with 1. 1 year GE, 2. 3 years with no-name financial planning outfit in Spain (do I have that right, another example of confusing account of job history) and 3. 1 year with a big Euro food company –lots of diverse experience in Europe. As to U.S. schools, I am not seeing this as H/S/W just based on the fact that there is no WOW factor unless you have not posted impressive extras, which would make you stand out there.

On the other hand, if you somehow got a 700+ GMAT, and you have extras, which are unlisted, well, maybe Harvard or Wharton. I just don't see Stanford somehow, unless your company is a feeder to them. The work pedigree is super important at HSW for International students, so this really counts for you. My guess is the Stanford admits with Spanish passports are all deeply pedigreed, as are the Stanford admits from Latin America (calling Cemex and the big IB's) of whom there are mucho. Your first job at GE was the right track for Stanford. The issue is how much pedigree your current employer has. Tuck and Kellogg certainly seem in the running, if you can get ~700 GMAT.

I think you would be a strong candidate at most Euro schools. For me, the Euro vs. USA question is pretty simple: Where do you want to work after getting your MBA? If in the USA, then you have to go to a U.S. school because any consulting company that scouts you at a Euro school is going to want to assign you to Europe. And my guess is, not many U.S. food giants recruit in Europe either.

Mr. Audit

- 720 GMAT
- 3.72 GPA
- Undergraduate degree in accounting and economics from Tel Aviv University
- Work experience includes three years of service in the Israeli defense force as an intelligence analyst; now work in the audit department of a Big Four firm in Israel focusing on SEC-regulated companies
- Extracurricular involvement as president of the university debating club, a team leader in Junior Achievement Israel, and also did a year of community service during which I was responsible for 100 children
- During my second year in school worked for 9 months as a Psychometric instructor, which is the Israeli equivalent to the SAT, following a 2% mark in that test.
- "Want to get your opinion about moving to the advisory services department – would that make any difference with my acceptance chances?"
- Goal: "Want an MBA in order to get into IB in the states."
- 25-year-old white male

Odds of Success:

Harvard: 20-30%
Wharton: 40+%
Columbia: 40+%
Chicago: 40+%
Kellogg: 40+%
NYU: 50%

Sandy's Analysis: It is true that Big Four accounting work in the U.S. is not as highly valued as pure strategy consulting, even for the strategy parts of the Big Four themselves. However, Big Four firms, even in audit alone, in

Europe and the Middle East are considered more selective, and U.S. schools are aware of that, especially in Russia and other parts of Eastern Europe.

All that said, if you can get out of audit and into some kind of advisory services, do that. Even if it means short gigs in both audit and advisory. Guys like you get into Wharton, Columbia, Kellogg, and Chicago and don't get in, depending on luck, execution, recommendations, and how you make this all add up. It is even permissible at those places to say you want to transition into finance and banking.

Although I would not say per se that you want to do investment banking in the U.S.

This is the identical issue I raised with the German guy in the first profile this week —you should not appear more interested in becoming a successful U.S. resident than you are in developing a passion for some substantive business idea or 'space.' In terms of applying, develop a passion for an idea and be willing to follow that wherever the chips fall. Say that you are interested in helping companies grow and that could take several forms, including finance, and your substantive interests are x, y z type companies —e.g. companies involved in energy in the Mid-East like 1, 2, and 3 and you admire leaders like Joe Blow, the CFO at Generic Mid-East Company and Joe Blow 2, an investment banker at Generic IB who has worked with companies like x, y, z.

That way it sounds like you are following some passion business schools admire. Given your army background as an analyst, you might say you are interested in high-tech investment banking in Middle East. Regardless of what you actually did, people will believe that an analyst in army intelligence = computers somehow. That story will work all over.

Your chances at HBS will turn on execution, etc. and what they think of the overseas version of your Big Four experience. As always, how many applicants from the Israeli and European offices of your firm go to HBS per year is an important stat.

For the record, Israeli passport holders at HBS per year now average seven versus three in the years 2001-04.

Mr. Saudi Arabia

- 700 GMAT
- 3.6 GPA
- Undergraduate degree in engineering from a public university in North Carolina
- Has nine years of experience in operations with the largest oil and gas company in the world, running an 85-employee division and a $120 million budget
- Have made a career change where I now advise management and develop company strategies "so I am badly in need of an MBA degree"
- Selected among the top 1% of 58,000 corporate employees
- Little extracurricular involvement
- 32 years old

Odds of Success:

Harvard Business School: 20%
Stanford: 10%
Wharton: 25%
MIT: 40%
Chicago: 40%
NYU: 40+%

Sandy's Analysis: HBS and Stanford do not take 32-year-old Oil Guys, and the Oil Guys they do take from Exxon, Shell, BP and Schlumberger usually have both high GPA and GMATs and some added factor about extras or do-gooder stuff. The fact you are leading tons of people and managing a budget of **XXXX** millions is actually a negative since it smells of an Executive MBA or some other program like the one-year Stanford/MIT Sloan Fellows program for mid-managers.

By saying your goal is "to take on more responsibility and future role. My degree will be sponsored by my company" you are positioning yourself for those programs and giving full-time MBA programs reasons to ding you, or more likely, write back or call you and suggest applying for the EMBA (they sometimes do that).

MIT itself, despite its Sloan Fellows program, might be impressed if they think you will add to their mix, and are not a nerd. Lack of extras, as Mr. Garcia, the adcom there, has stated, is not an issue for him. Wharton could admit you because they run older, you got a lot to offer, and the fact you will be employed after graduation and don't need any scholarship is always a plus.

As to Chicago and NYU, you are not their main meal, but they could find you an attractive side dish, and the numbers all add up, including no need to give you any scholarship.

Mr. Olympian

- 710 GMAT
- 3.4 GPA
- Undergraduate degree in European Studies from unknown European university
- Some eight years of work as a full-time athlete, captain, Olympic Medalist, who co-owns a gym.
- Extracurricular activities include outreach and coaching children under a sports foundation. Volunteer to help disadvantaged adults.
- 30-years-old
- Goals: Business development or general management

Odds of Success:

Wharton: 40%
Chicago: 50+%
Kellogg: 50+%
Michigan: 60%
Duke: 60%
Yale: 50%
INSEAD: 60+%

Sandy's Analysis: I'm as impressed by an Olympic medal as the next guy but why do you want an MBA? You say "business development or general management" but what does that mean? You already own a gym. The guy who owns the gym I go to has a Porsche Panamera in a reserved spot ahead of the ones for handicapped people and real bad taste in music to judge what they play while I do my time on the schlep-mill. Agreed, I am not the target audience, but how about some Bruce Hornsby or Eagles classics?

You need to reposition your goals as transitioning to an executive role in some NGO involving sports/kids/relief/development. Sorry if that is what you meant. In that case the story changes dramatically, and you are not an ex-Olympian trying to get some job with Anheuser-Busch (home of many jocky type execs, although not at your level) but someone with a very powerful story. Go light on the gym. Most people dislike gym owners for many, many reasons, including complex contracts with hidden fees and for their failure to control the lunks (real word, well, sorta, look it up) etc. it's like phone company. You have a great story and assuming you can put it together, the 710 and your medals could make you a contender.

Wharton may go for this on a day they get tired of seeing the usual. Booth and Kellogg are genuinely predisposed to like guys like you, and other places are kind of in line. So, good luck. I'm rooting for you. Just get story real straight. Find MBA's who are running do-gooder sports-related organizations and say they are your role models.

Mr. Impact Investor &
Ms. Indian First Generation

(Engaged couple both applying to B-school)

Mr. Impact Investor

- 720 GMAT
- 3.2 GPA
- Undergraduate degree in electronics and communication engineering from a non-Indian Institute of Technology engineering college in India
- 3.8 Graduate GPA
- Masters degree in finance from a top Indian university
- Work experience includes two years as an investment banking analyst at a bulge bracket Wall Street firm, a year in the development practice of a Big Four firm, and a year and one-half at the private investment arm of the World Bank
- Lots of extracurricular involvement including leader of Cricket team
- Won Best Research Project Award for a paper published in the Institute of Electrical and Electronics Engineer journal.
- 29 years old
- Goal is to work in venture capital or private equity and to eventually start an "impact investment firm"

First Generation

- 710 GMAT
- 4.0 GPA
- Undergraduate degree in business from a top Indian university
- 4.0 Graduate GPA
- Graduate degree in finance

- Started and ran for two years a small venture creating accessories and gift items, employing women from marginalized communities
- Currently working for three years at a leading global credit rating agency. Also working on firm's strategy with the CEO.
- Heavy extracurricular involvement, including founding member of an alumni advisory council
- 24 years old
- Goal to work in consulting before setting out on her own

Odds of Success:

Harvard: 40% to 60%
Stanford: 40% to 60%
Wharton: 60+%
MIT: 60+%
Chicago: 60+%
Kellogg: 60+%
Dartmouth: 60+%
Columbia: 50+%

Sandy's Analysis: Just in general, couples are not treated as packages, and a super strong partner cannot drag in a less attractive partner (from the school's perspective), especially at Harvard, Stanford or Wharton.

The one big exception is the Wait List. If one of you is naturally in, and the other is on the WL, and it is about late June, what the hell, schools often say, "We may as well take the spouse versus any of the other single and uncommitted and callow clods on the WL. After all, who cares anyway and couples make the world go round."

At schools outside of H/S/W this may vary a bit, and the magnetism of the stronger applicant can sometimes help the weaker one, especially if the weaker partner is not chopped liver to begin with. As to how being 'partners' or 'significant others' and not legally married impacts this, well, a bit, in some fuzzy way. To the extent you appear to be married in terms of duration, commitment, etc, and can demonstrate that, the better.

Being engaged, well, when is the marriage? Although I understand Indian couples don't often run off to city hall.

As to Impact Investor, the future hubby, it's sloppy but this is real strong based on super duper extras, World Bank branding (Is that your current gig? That's important), research interests (not that schools care about research, and in some ways too much is a negative. If you sound like a Finance PhD or even Business PhD material, and you don't want to sound like that, especially given the M.A. degree, so make sure that doesn't happen). But in your case, the jobs and research bleach out the impact of lowish grades and non-IIT. World Bank experience and World Bank type goals are a real plus at H/S/W, especially in your case when coupled with bulge bracket experience in India.

This just all adds up to a smart, committed, impactful guy—and that story works at H/S/W if you execute correctly, which in your case means not sounding like a future PhD, and if you can get some semi big deal to back you. Age is maybe one or two years off, but they may blink at that.

As to First Generation, the future wife.

Okay, in general, credit rating gigs (Moody's, S&P, and Fitch) are not considered selective jobs by H/S/W but are, similar to Big Four gigs, an acceptable place to find minorities or other off-the-grid stories. That being said, such jobs outside the U.S. held by internationals (both credit rating and Big Four) are considered more selective because, well, they are.

In your case, you are 1) International, 2) First gen college, 3) Have classy other jobs, even if odd in terms of timing, 4) Have a compelling do-gooder business story, and 5) Lots of extras. Plus the 4.0 GPA (twice) is the clincher. GMAT is fine, and a non-issue.

Lots to like. Applicants like you get into H/S/W, depending on execution, luck, and maybe having some big shot at the Credit Shop go to bat for you, which is possible since you appear to be working with the CEO. This just has the whiff of a winner. So chances are good at H/S/W (40% to 70%) and even higher at other places, but you will need to, especially at Tuck, Columbia, Booth and Kellogg, convince them you really want to come.

Maybe, there's some synergy with your husband, since both stories dovetail a bit, in terms of lots of extras and social impact. An adcom might correctly get a vibe you two would be a real plus on campus. That could especially help at Tuck (which is friendly and couple-y) and MIT (which always needs high-performing non-nerds).

Mr. IIT

- 740 GMAT
- 3.2 GPA (in U.S. terms)
- Undergraduate degree from the Indian Institute of Technology
- Work experience at near Ivy management consulting firm
- Extracurricular involvement includes student president and festival convener

> **Odds of Success:**
>
> Harvard Business School: Less than 30%
> Stanford: Less than 20%
> Wharton: 30%
> Dartmouth: 40% to 50%
> Chicago: 50% to 60%

Sandy's Analysis: First off, IIT grades do not translate fairly into GPA by some formulas. IIT kids really need to stress class standing, especially if you are in the top 10 percent of your class. Always report that along with your grades. Schools say they are aware of this, but who knows. Some schools just blindly follow the formulas of agencies, which claim to be specialists in translating international grades. Those places often strike me as the 300-pound ladies on the sex chat lines. Who knows who is whispering into Dee Leopold's ear that your U.S. GPA is 3.5? A world expert or the next contestant on Slumdog Millionnaire? That is a worthy topic of discussion.

All that said, IIT males (versus females which is quite rare) with low grades and non-McKinsey/Bain/BCG/Monitor consulting gigs who do not have some ace current extracurriculars serving victims, etc., as a rule do not get into Harvard or Stanford. Wharton takes guys like you, depending on your age, execution, and luck. And your chances down the totem pole of business schools go up.

Your college extras are fine to me, but schools will give you less credit unless you were doing something like helping poor people and victims. I don't know what 'fest convener' is, but it doesn't sound like working in a leper colony or even helping poor kids learn math. Chances at Wharton, Tuck and Booth are solid depending on execution.

Mr. Palestinian

- 690 GMAT
- 2.8 GPA (Willing to take all four of the classes I received a D in over again from local colleges if that would help)
- Undergraduate degree from a state college
- Work experience includes six years as manager of a small generic pharmaceutical wholesale company with eight employees, including telecommuting workers. After selling that business, I now manage an independent retail pharmacy and run a website which involves personal shopping and international shipping to customers in the Middle East
- Extracurricular involvement as a volunteer teaching English to immigrants
- Son of Palestinian refugees who is the first and only person in my family to graduate high school and college
- Fluent in Arabic, having lived in Jordan for five years
- Goal: To work for an American company that does business in the Middle East or to start his own consulting company for American businesses that want to do business in the Middle East
- 29-year-old Palestinian living in New York and completely bald

Odds of Success:

Harvard: 5%
Stanford: 5%
Wharton: 5%
Kellogg, Booth, Duke, Virginia: 20%
Boston University: 30% to 40+%
Boston College: 30% to 40+%
Maryland: 50+%
Babson: 50+%

Sandy's Analysis: Being bald won't play much of a factor, and I don't hold it against you since I'm in comb-over mode myself.

OK, moving on . . . I would retake those courses you got a "D" in, especially if they were "quanty," (e.g. stats, economics, algebra) just as a show of good faith that you are serious about applying and can still sit for 45-to-85 minute blocks of time and regurgitate . . . whatever . . . which is a good proxy for business school, despite all the superficial changes they yap about. This could be especially important if your GMAT split was low on the Quant side.

You've got a compelling personal story, obviously, and certified Palestinian refugees are a valued addition to the campus mix at all business schools—that, and being the first in your family to achieve higher education. The weak part of your story is what appears to be working in two small family businesses: the small generic pharma company and now retail pharmacy and website.

I salute you, and the world may need more pharmacies than investment banks, but the B-schools don't quite see it that way. They look for diamonds in the rough like you to have gotten lucky once before they agree to pick you up. In your case, that would have meant somehow excelling at college and getting a real Blue Chip job for a consulting company or a bank or Big 4 which are nursing grounds for raw talent. Or just doing OK in college and then getting a break through a college alumnus and getting some kind standard job at a retail bank, insurance company, or local business.

The trouble with your jobs is that schools have no way to judge them. The fact that you were running a generic pharma wholesale company with eight employees, some of whom were telecommuting, might in reality be an amazing enterprise for you and your family. But schools may suspect it was some kind of dodgy pill mill—especially since it was sold and you then opened pharmacy, which seems like a downward progression.

Just giving this to you straight. I totally salute your family's efforts and struggles. OK, maybe I am being too cynical, but I don't see this as

Harvard, Stanford or Wharton, for sure. And I think you will find it hard, if not impossible, at other schools typically ranked in the Top 10 for the same reasons: low GPA, only family business work history and no 'standard jobs', etc. Given your OK GMAT score, and if you do take those D courses over again, you might stand a chance at more "regional"-focused business schools, such as Pace in New York, Babson, Boston University, the University of Maryland, Penn State, Michigan State, Boston College, UT-Dallas, et al.

It is not clear how much good those places can do in helping you meet your dreams of working for an American company in the U.S. that does business in the Middle East, unless you already have contacts at such companies. You really have to check out what hiring is like at those schools, especially for kids who don't come from the area or have prior connections with employers. A lot of those schools are feeders to regional banks, and it helps to come from the, well, region.

If anyone knows more about hiring at schools like that, please check in.

If you want to start your own consulting company, and have pre-existing contacts, schools like that can certainly teach you basic business skills, and often do a better job at it than Top 10 schools, in fact. You might also check out a school like Babson in Massachusetts, which is focused on students who want to start companies.

Mr. Lawyer

- 640 GMAT (suffer from severe ADHD)
- 3.4 GPA
- Law degree from Tel Aviv University
- Work experience includes two and one-half years as a junior associate in the largest law firm in Israel, five years as the manager of a competitive tennis club, four years as an agent in the Prime Minister's office, and three years of military service in the intelligence corps
- Extracurricular involvement includes the founding of a non-profit tennis program for underprivileged children, also offered legal assistance to those without means and currently teach elementary children from Ethiopia
- Short-term Goal: To join an energy/infrastructure company
- Long-term Goal: To further develop family business (infrastructure consulting) and merge with a large corporation
- 29-year-old male

Odds of Success:

MIT: 10%
Michigan: 20%
Chicago: 15%
Berkeley: 10%
Duke: 20%
Cornell: 20%

Sandy's Analysis: Here is some tough love–retake the GMAT, either with accommodations, if they give it for ADHD or with medication, or with luck. Keep taking it until you get a 680+ if that is possible. I cannot really puzzle out your career path or the timing of when you did what, or what exactly you are doing now, or if you are mixing extracurrics and full-time jobs.

Maybe it is one guy with ADHD (me, non-clinical, just extreme impatience) trying to make sense of scrambled account of another guy with same. Are you currently doing this full-time: "Today teach Elementary School Children of Ethiopian origin theories in law." Or is that an extra? Or is that what you are doing? Anyway, it is not all that important to sort this out. If your family business is BIG enough, some school might let you in, if you make a plausible case that you want to transform it and they believe you.

Otherwise, no offense, but this crazy-quilt career path and age and low-ish GPA and GMAT make you a real tough sell. I'd be very creative about how you describe your career so far, stressing the traditional stuff like Army and working for the government, and lawyering, and going light on managing tennis clubs. Then, really stress what you plan to do with family business AND DO NOT SAY SELL IT. You don't need an MBA for that. Being a lawyer should be enough to at least put you in touch with other smart lawyers who do stuff like that.

Mr. P&G

- 770 GMAT
- 2.5 GPA (top 5% of my peers)
- Undergraduate degree in engineering from a top engineering school in Spain
- Work experience includes five years with Procter & Gamble in Spain, half as a business analyst on a business development team and half as a marketing manager; also worked for six months in France in R&D
- Extracurricular involvement includes the leading the university drama club for several years, slight collaboration with NGOs
- Goal: To acquire business knowledge to set up my own company.
- 29-year-old Spanish male

Odds of Success:

Harvard: 40+%
Stanford: 10% to 30%
MIT: 50+%
Northwestern: 50+%
Chicago: 50+%
NYU: 50%*

*all premised on your claim that a 2.5 GPA at your top school in Spain is also in the top 5 percent. Otherwise, all bets are off.

Sandy's Analysis: You really, really need to prove that a 2.5 GPA is also in the top 5% of your class, if that is what you are saying above. Get the registrar of your university to make that clear. This is absolutely critical.

After that, this brightens considerably: We got a 770 GMAT, and five years at P&G, a company all B-schools respect. Play up the NGO connections or build them up. The rest of your extras are all college stuff, and while interesting, they don't impact adcoms much, especially since you are now 29. Guys at P&G are expected to have more extras because it is not exactly like working at an Investment Bank in terms of spare time.

OK, all that said, HBS and Stanford take P&G guys, even older ones, and especially from Spain, which is not a frequent supplier of admits. For example, in a typical HBS class there will be seven to eight kids from Spain versus 12 from France and 14 from Germany (and five from Portugal). Most of those Spaniards will be from Blue Chip companies like yours or international IB and consulting companies. I'd say your chances at Stanford are weak because there is no do-gooder jive driving you in, and they are less interested in international P&G–type applicants per se, versus using companies like P&G as a source of talented minority candidates (along with Big 4 auditing companies).

HBS is bigger and feels a kinship with P&G in terms of size and age. So chances there are better, although age and lack of extras could be an issue. MIT will just about admit anyone with a 770 GMAT with a pulse who can also make a credible case that they want to come, which actually might be difficult for you because although you say you want to start a business – which they like – you don't have much cred in that field given your resume and long-ish history of working for a "stodgy" company.

Kellogg will go for you and so too will Chicago just based on marketing background and stats (again, assuming you get a YouTube tape of Registrar of your University swearing on a Bible that 2.5 is top 5 percent). I might tell those places you are interested in product management and marketing and not starting your own company so you don't sound like a burn-out, which is a real issue with a story and too-long career like yours.

Mr. Credit Card

- 750 GMAT
- No GPA but graduated in the top 8% of my class
- Undergraduate degree in economy from the best university in Argentina
- Work Experience includes over five years at American Express starting "as a junior doing elemental things" and now lead three teams—in operations, customer retention, and customer acquisition
- Have won several prizes at Amex, including the Will to Win Award, the Customer Service Award, and the Outstanding Achievements Award (regional prize). Also, I was nominated by Latam region to the Worldwide Customer Service Award two times, and to the Chairman Award of Innovation once.
- Extracurricular involvement as the leader of a basketball team which has won the local tournament twice and the national tournament once. Also taught guitar lessons for three years after studying the instrument for six years.
- Goal: To land a management consulting job at BCG, Bain or McKinsey
- 26-year-old Argentine male

Odds of Success:

Harvard: 15% to 20%
Stanford: 10% to 15%
Wharton: 30% to 40+%
Columbia: 30% to 50+%
Northwestern: 30% to 50+%
Dartmouth: 30% to 40+%
NYU: 40% to 50+%

Sandy's Analysis: As to Harvard and Stanford, a lot will depend on what they think of your job at Amex. There is a term in admissions, 'credit card database jockey' and it describes techie guys who scour a credit card company's database looking for ways to increase fees, late charges, eliminate really poor deadbeats (who cannot pay and may declare bankruptcy or just disappear) and increase only so-so poor near-deadbeats who can pay the late fees (that is sweet spot, the favorite customer of all for credit card companies).

Sounds like you do a bit of that and maybe something more. You don't seem to be the disc jockey but the station manager and that could be a key difference.

And as I have noted several times, a B-rated job in the U.S. is often an A job in Eastern Europe of Latin America, viz. working for a Big Four accounting firm (OK but not great in New York, hard job to get in Moscow, and credited as such by B schools). So that part of the international currency exchange for B school jobs may help you. Your extras (basketball team and personal hobbies) are fine with me, but they are not the 'do-gooder, social-impact-beyond-yourself' gigs that turn-on HBS and Stanford.

I'm having a hard time getting a feel for the company awards you list, but if those are truly extraordinary and rare, and you have leaders in the company who strongly back your application, that could turn the tide. Otherwise, I am not seeing this as HBS or Stanford, although that is just a vibe I am getting from the whole story. Feel free to write back and tell me I am wrong.

A 750 GMAT is rare in Latin America, and I'm taking you at your word that you are in the top 8% of your class in the best university in the country. HBS takes five to six kids a year from Argentina, and they often have stats like yours, or U.S. schooling, and jobs in Blue Chip consulting firms and banks. Amex is sorta one step below that, but depending on what you do, and how it is perceived, you could be closer to real blue chip or farther away. Once again, the key question: Has anyone who did your job at Amex in the past five years applied to business school and what were the outcomes?

Once we get past HBS and Stanford, your situation is much better. Wharton and Columbia will go for your solid stats (high GPA and GMAT) and may have a more benign view of credit card company maestros. They also are not as enamored with do-gooder jive as HBS and Stanford. Tuck is in range for you as well, based on stats, and your general likeability, if indeed you come off that way if you visit. Kellogg will go for the stats as well as the Argentina connection.

Mr. Hedge Fund

- 760 GMAT
- Undergraduate degree in economics from a top three university in the United Kingdom
- Work experience includes one year in principal investments at a top investment bank and two years at a well-known hedge fund
- Pre-MBA compensation: EUR 150-250K
- Extracurricular involvement includes some school mentorship activities, and on the board of a few companies we are invested in
- Goal: "I currently work in Europe and plan to return here, doing a similar thing to what I'm doing now but with more (and eventually portfolio manager level) responsibilities. Would like to go to business school to expand my global network (which I feel will be useful at the PM level)"
- 26-year-old under-represented minority (Black)

Odds of Success:

Harvard Business School only: 40+%

Sandy's Analysis: I am assuming your current job is with the hedge fund. A lot of your HBS chances will turn on what HBS thinks of your employers, both the IB and the Hedge Fund. And the best way to figure that out is to find out the track record of those companies sending applicants to HBS over the past three to five years. As to Hedge Funds, especially, all hedge funds are not created equal, and its record in sending applicants to top schools, and some degree, its record of hiring Harvard MBAs after graduation really color the HBS adcom outlook.

As to being a URM [Under-Represented Minority), at HBS (and all U.S. schools), that term technically applies to only U.S. citizens, which does not seem to be you. Those schools in the first instance are concerned with forms they have to file with the U.S. Department of Whatever (Education, Civil Rights?) which headcounts the percentage of students who are 1. U.S. citizens, and 2. Either: A) Afro-American, B) Hispanic surname, C) from Puerto Rico, or D) Native American. So when you see that X percent of HBS class is "minority," that is what the number means–the total of those four groups.

All that said, the fact you are black, even if citizenship is U.K., is a plus, since it impacts your experiences and interests, and there are just not that many black males from anyplace with a 760 GMAT.

I would do a better dog-and-pony show on your goals, although you might just be "blah, blahing" to me and you already knew that. But your stated goals of planning to return to work in Europe aren't all that compelling: "Doing a similar thing to what I'm doing now but with more (and eventually Portfolio Manager level) responsibilities. Would like to go to business school to expand my global network (which I feel will be useful at the PM level)." HBS recognizes that what you are saying motivates many private equity and finance types to apply, but they don't enjoy hearing it back quite that insouciantly.

You need to puff it up so it sounds like HBS will be a transformational experience, help you become an impact investor, transform investments in areas 1, 2, 3. Also portfolio manager is not a favored Harvard endpoint in life. Well, not a favored HBS Adcom endpoint. Their thinking is, you don't really need an MBA for that, although many portfolio managers might disagree.

Being on company boards is good, although not quite an "extracurricular activity," as HBS understands the term. Nonetheless, OK experience for one essay. Your pre-MBA compensation of 150-250k Euros is probably on the high-end, even for PE applicants, but not a head-scratcher–just don't brag about it. At some compensation point, ~$500 U.S.D., schools begin to wonder why you are applying, but not yet.

I don't often say this, but a good deal of your outcome will turn on execution. Both how you position goals, and how likeable and, ahem, 'emotionally intelligent' you appear in essays. HBS dings and admits lots of guys like you, and sometimes it is hard to figure out what the decision turned on. Guys like you who get dinged and get feedback from Dee Leopold as part of her Ding-A-Thon phone sessions, often hear, "nothing really 'wrong' etc. which means 1. You blew the interview in some subtle way, 2. Essays and total picture where not likeable, for reasons very difficult to articulate (too banal, too braggy, annoying 'voice.')

Ms. Marine Biologist

- 680 GMAT
- 3.48 GPA
- Undergraduate degree in marine biology from a Canadian university with a minor in business
- Work experience includes six years as a purser aboard a large super yacht, assisting with a $7 to $10 million budget, human resources, concierge and itinerary planning for Forbes Top 100 clientele; also seven months working for a new research vessel non-profit company specializing in oceanographic research.
- Goal: Shifting career into finance
- 30-year-old Canadian female

Odds of Success:

London Business School: 40+%
University of Western Ontario: 50+%
Sauder School of Business: 50+%

Sandy's Analysis: If there is any profession that can top even architecture in terms of being "cool," it is marine biology. Think I'm kidding? Read this college application essay from Rachel, <u>on my website</u>, in the famous "Worst College Essays Ever Written Section." She wants to be a pediatric (baby) marine biologist because the profession is so cool, and as she says,

I like the ocean, small things, and animals. :-) . . .

By the way, I was looking in your course catalog for the marine biologist courses and those courses seem to involve working with fish or things like fish. :-(

I'm not really all that interested in fish, I mean I'll take the required fish courses, but what I am really interested in is animals that live in or near the water, except fish. :-(

I like seals, especially baby seals, :-)

Of course, you did Rachel two better since 1) You actually got a marine biology degree and then 2), You avoided real fish and baby seals altogether by, in your own words, being a purser "onboard a large Super Yacht. Assisting with a $7-10 million budget, human resources, concierge and itinerary planning services for Forbes Top 100 clientele . . ." Oh boy, fat cats at sea . . .if only those life preservers could talk .

I assume you have heard all the <u>Gilligan's Island</u> jokes, or maybe that show is before your time or banned in Canada.

OK, let's get back on terra firma: you're 30, have an OK GPA from some boutique marine biology college which probably the Canadian business schools you mention have heard of – and for any other B-school, well, it's marine biology! After the mist clears, basically you have been performing some hands-on accounting and project planning services for what I take is a small company, e.g. the owner of the Super Yacht.

That, plus the marine biology halo effect should be solid enough for the schools you are interested in if you can make a case as to why you want an MBA. Your stated reasons, that you want to "switch into finance," really needs to be honed into some story which captures your past and makes sense in terms of being able to get that job when you graduate.

As noted before, goal statements are half image projection, half fantasy, and half due diligence about the chosen profession and how a school can help you as well. Yup, that is three halves and good goal statements are that dense. You need to capture some or all of those elements into yours.

It is unclear from your profile which job you currently have, the non-profit gig or the Super Yacht job? Assuming it is the Fat Cat job, you need to somehow project those skills into a plausible job at X, Y or Z and say that is what you want to do post-MBA, and that is why you need the degree. X, Y, and Z need to be jobs which 1. Often require an MBA, and 2. Somehow engage with what you have done prior, even if it is a stretch, adcoms like continuity blended with change rather than naked change. Just off the top of my head here, you might say you are interested in the intersection of finance and hospitality and leisure (since that broadly speaking was your Fat Cat Ocean gig). Then find some people with MBA's who work in that field via Google or Linked-In, and use them as role models. If you really want to max this out, find the 5 biggest hospitality and leisure operators in Canada and sniff around for potential jobs there. Sure, it's artificial hokum but it reads well in an application.

General note: it just amazes me how often kids writing B-school apps somehow forget about Google —a tool they would turn to 100 times a day for trivia. That same search came up with a .pdf from Deloitte Consulting about trends in the Canadian hospitality industry—written in French! Pas moi, but maybe our marine biologist can read it.

One next to last thing: You may also have to explain why, given your age and experience, you are not applying for an Executive MBA. Finally, I am not sure I see the case for someone like you going to school in London. You really should do some homework about where grads at London Business School get jobs, especially if you want to stay in Canada.

ABOUT THE AUTHORS

John A. Byrne

John A. Byrne is the Founder and Editor-in-Chief of PoetsandQuants.com and C-Change Media Inc., its parent company based in Corte Madera, California. He first began reporting and writing about business school education in the 1980s and created the first regularly published rankings of full-time MBA programs for BusinessWeek magazine in 1988. For many years, he covered business schools for BusinessWeek, setting up its online presence for the magazine in 1994 and authoring several editions of BusinessWeek's Guides to The Best Business Schools.

In August of 2010, he launched PoetsandQuants.com as the first in a network of websites owned and operated by C-Change Media. Within 18 months, P&Q was generating more than one million monthly page views and had become a cult favorite of applicants to the world's most prestigious business schools. PoetsandQuantsforExecs.com, a website devoted to the coverage of executive education and Executive MBA programs, was launched in February of 2011. TippingTheScales.com, for applicants to the world's prestige law schools, is currently being readied for launch.

Until Nov. of 2009, Byrne had been executive editor and editor-in-chief of BusinessWeek.com. He led BusinessWeek.com to record levels of reader engagement and traffic, oversaw the redesign of the site, and launched extensive new areas of coverage on management and lifestyle. Mr. Byrne initiated the site's twice-daily executive news summary, weekly interactive case studies, multi-media classroom videos, as well as new blogs and podcasts.

Under his leadership, BusinessWeek.com had won two consecutive National Magazine Awards, the most prestigious recognition in magazine publishing, an EPpy for Best Business Website with over one million unique visitors (over The Wall Street Journal), and second place honors as the Best Website of the Year for news and business by the Magazine Publishers Association. In 2008 alone, BW.com captured an unprecedented 21 awards and nominations for journalism excellence. His weekly podcast on Business Week's cover story has been downloaded more than 10 million times. Mr. Byrne's views on the future of journalism have made him a popular speaker and essayist. In recent years, he has spoken at more than a dozen conferences, has been frequently interviewed about the new world of journalism, and has been published by Harvard University's Nieman Reports, The Christian Science Monitor, and MediaWeek magazine.

Prior to role at BusinessWeek.com, he was the executive editor for the print publication since 2005, during which he began three new annual franchises, including the highly successful Customer Service Champions and the Best Places to Launch a Career, and recruited to the magazine such popular weekly columnists as Jack and Suzy Welch, Maria Bartiromo, and renown wine critic Robert Parker. He also helped to recruit numerous writers and editors to the magazine staff, including its first Assistant Managing Editor for investigative coverage, a senior editor for finance, a management editor, and several senior writers.

Previously, Mr. Byrne was editor-in-chief of *Fast Company* magazine. He joined *Fast Company* in April 2003, succeeding founding editors Alan Webber and Bill Taylor, where he worked to reinvent the business magazine. Under his leadership, Fast Company won many coveted journalism awards, including its first Gerald Loeb award, the highest honor in business journalism. Mr. Byrne also made Fast Company the first business brand to launch an online blog and created, through a partnership with Monitor Group, an annual award competition for social entrepreneurs. More importantly, Mr. Byrne found and cultivated a buyer for the magazine, resulting in a $35 million purchase that saved the publication from an almost certain closure.

Before joining Fast Company, he worked for BusinessWeek for nearly 18 years, largely in the position of Senior Writer and authoring a record 57 cover stories for the magazine. His articles have explored the fairness of executive pay, the folly of management fads, and the governance of major corporations. Mr. Byrne's magazine writing has won numerous awards and has been republished in collections of the best writing on business. He was named a National Magazine Award finalist as well as a Gerald Loeb award finalist twice. Among his more widely recognized cover stories are "Philip Morris: Inside America's Most Reviled Company," a provocative exploration of the men who ran the largest tobacco corporation in the world, "The Fall of a Dot-Com," an investigative story on how big-name investors, blinded by Net fever, poured millions into a dot-com that fell into bankruptcy, "Joe Berardino's Fall from Grace," a narrative of how Arthur Andersen's CEO presided over the demise of his legendary firm, "The Man Who Invented Management," a reflective essay on why management guru Peter Drucker's ideas still matter, and "Are CEOs Paid Too Much?," an early examination (1992) of why executive compensation was out-of-control.

Mr. Byrne developed the idea of a monthly best-sellers list, launched the industry-leading business school rankings, established and managed the magazine's ranking of the best and worst corporate boards, and created its annual list of the most generous philanthropists. He also built out the business education franchise online in the mid-1990s, setting the stage for a highly regarded online community and one that has reaped millions of dollars in annual revenue for BusinessWeek. He has been a frequent commentator on television, having appeared on CNN's Moneyline and CNBC's Squawk Box and Business Center.

Mr. Byrne is the author or co-author of ten books on business, leadership, and management, including two national bestsellers. World Changers, published by Penguin Books' Portfolio imprint in December of 2011, is his first book in ten years. His previous book, published Sept. 11, 2001 by Warner Books, was Jack: Straight from the Gut, the highly anticipated collaboration with former General Electric Co. CEO Jack Welch. The book debuted at the very top of The New York Times bestseller list and remained on the list for 26 consecutive weeks. Mr. Byrne has written or co-authored seven other books, including Chainsaw (HarperCollins, 1999), the behind-the-scenes story of Al Dunlap's rise and fall as a business celebrity. The book received widespread acclaim. Publishers Weekly called the book a "blistering saga" and a "sizzling tale." The Street.com said Chainsaw "should be required reading in all business and accounting schools."

Mr. Byrne's other books include: Informed Consent (McGraw-Hill, 1995); The Headhunters (MacMillan, 1986); Odyssey (Harper & Row, 1987), the business biography of former Apple Computer chairman John Sculley; and The Whiz Kids (Currency/Doubleday, 1993), which explored the life and times of ten Army Air Force officers who helped to remake the Ford Motor Co. in the post-war period. Managment guru Tom Peters called The Whiz Kids "an important milestone in American management analysis." Warren Bennis has said the book is "the best history of American business from World War II to the present." Mr. Byrne also wrote BusinessWeek's Guide to the Best Business Schools (McGraw-Hill, 1989, 1990, 1993, 1995, and 1997) and co-wrote BusinessWeek's Guide to the Best Executive Education Programs (McGraw-Hill, 1992).

Mr. Byrne joined Business Week in 1985 from Forbes magazine where he served as an associate editor and staff writer for four years. He previously worked as a correspondent for Fairchild Publications in London, as bureau chief, and in Washington, D.C., where he covered the U.S. Supreme Court, Congress, and several regulatory agencies.

Sanford Kreisberg

Sandy Kreisberg, the founder and president of HBSGuru.com as well as The Cambridge Essay Service, has helped well over a thousand MBA applicants get into leading programs at Harvard Business School, Stanford, Wharton, MIT Sloan, Columbia and others since 1995.

The former director of communications at the MIT Sloan School, Kreisberg taught expository writing at Harvard University for eight years from 1980 until 1988, specializing in the personal essay. He also earned an M.A. at Harvard in English Literature in 1971.

Kreisberg has been offering his advice to MBA applicants at PoetsandQuants. com since June of 2011. He is frequently cited by The Wall Street Journal, The New York Times, The Economist and The Harvard Crimson as an expert in business school admissions. He has appeared on the Today Show and was interviewed by The Economist for its 2007 Business School Forum. Sandy's Q&A blog on Business Week magazine's B-School Forum has over 16,000 posts and is the most viewed blog of over several hundred on that forum.